Tongue Fu!

Tongue Fu!

Sam Horn

ST. MARTIN'S PRESS
NEW YORK

Design by Sara Stemen

Library of Congress Cataloging-in-Publication Data

Horn, Sam.
    Tongue Fu! : how to deflect, disarm, and defuse any verbal conflict / by
Sam Horn. — 1st ed.
        p.   cm.
    Includes bibliographical references.
    ISBN 0-312-14054-1
    1. Verbal self-defense.   2. Interpersonal conflict.
3. Interpersonal communication.   I. Title.
    BF637.V47H67   1996
    153.6—dc20   95-41254
                                                                    CIP

First edition: February 1996

10 9 8 7 6 5 4 3 2 1

May this book serve as a living legacy
to my parents, Warren and Ruth Reed,
who served as the original source and role model for these
principles . . .
and to my sons, Tom and Andrew Horn,
who I hope will use these ideas
so they experience life as a blessing, not a burden.

· Contents ·

"BE WEALTHY IN YOUR FRIENDS."

—WILLIAM SHAKESPEARE

I have indeed been wealthy in my friends, and I want to thank several pivotal people who helped make *Tongue Fu!* a reality.

Dr. Ray Oshiro, University of Hawaii program specialist, for supporting my speaking career from the beginning, and for steering me on this path in 1989 by asking me to develop a course on dealing with difficult people.

Karen Waggoner, valued executive director of Action Seminars, for taking care of business and for teaching me all about synergy. Two heads (when one of them is Karen's) are definitely better than one!

John and Shannon Tullius, founders/directors of the Maui Writers Conference, for having the vision to create this world-class event which catapulted my writing career.

Michael Larsen and Elizabeth Pomada, literary agents par extraordinaire and much-appreciated patron saints, for kicking back this proposal several times and asking, "Is this the best you can do?"

Jennifer Enderlin of St. Martin's Press, every writer's dream editor, for her enthusiasm and persistence on behalf of this project.

And to my sister, Cheri Grimm. Mahalo for being the constant in my life. I treasure our forty-plus-year journey together and your ever-present support.

· Introduction ·

Are you curious as to how this book got started?

In 1989, Dr. Ray Oshiro, a continuing education program specialist, asked me to present a public workshop on dealing with difficult people for the University of Hawaii. We had both noticed the same trend: Organizations were increasingly requesting training to help their employees learn how to cope with rude customers and uncooperative coworkers.

In creating the curriculum for this course, I realized why most people are woefully unprepared to handle difficult behavior. Conflict resolution is not taught in school along with history, math, and science. As a result, people don't know what to do or say when someone mistreats them. They often end up RIK (Retaliating in Kind) or SIS (Suffering in Silence). Neither reaction helps.

My goal was to develop real-life responses people could use immediately to handle the challenges they face on a daily basis. I didn't want to waste time on theories. Platitudes don't help much when someone's yelling at you or blaming you for something that's not your fault.

I knew I was on the right track one hour into that first seminar. At our morning break, one of the attendees didn't leave his chair.

He just sat there slowly nodding his head, gazing off into the distance. I walked over and asked him what he was thinking about. He said, "Sam, I'm a real estate broker. Several of my clients are extremely demanding and arrogant. They seem to think they can treat me any way they want, and I'm tired of it. I took this course to learn some zingers to fire back and put them in their place. That's not what this is about, is it?"

Glad that he had grasped the essence of the course so quickly, I agreed. "You're right. When people are being difficult, it doesn't help to get back, get mad, or get even."

He went on: "I'm a student of martial arts. I've studied karate, Tai Chi, aikido, and judo. What you're suggesting is the *verbal* equivalent of kung fu, isn't it?" I said, "That's true. It's kind of like . . . *tongue fu!*" We looked at each other and burst out laughing. Eureka! The perfect name.

Since then, I've offered several hundred workshops for a wide variety of groups from Young President Organization executives and IRS auditors to members of the Honolulu police department. Participants have asked for a book on the subject, saying they want to take these ideas home, read them again and again, and share them with friends, family, and coworkers.

AN OVERVIEW OF TONGUE FU!

"There are no victims without volunteers." —ANONYMOUS

The purpose of kung fu (a Chinese martial art emphasizing internal development) is to defuse, disarm, or deflect someone's *physical* attack. The purpose of Tongue Fu! (a mental art emphasizing internal development) is to defuse, disarm, or deflect someone's *psychological* attack. It is a spoken form of self-defense—the constructive alternative to giving a tongue-lashing or to being tongue tied.

The goal of Tongue Fu! is to learn how to conduct yourself with confidence so you keep from being abused verbally. If provoked, however, you will be able to use these martial arts for the mind and mouth to skillfully protect yourself. Never again will you have a mental meltdown and feel helpless in the face of aggression.

Tongue Fu! is not just about handling unfair or unkind behavior. It's more a philosophy of life, a way to communicate that can help you get along better with everyone both on and off the job. You'll learn how to prevent conflicts and produce cooperation and how to *choose* to stay kind even if others are being inconsiderate or cruel.

No one enjoys dealing with difficult people, yet it is an everyday part of life. These ideas can help you skillfully disarm disagreeable people so your personal and professional relationships are less stressful and more enjoyable. You'll learn dozens of clever, noncombative comebacks so you can speak up for yourself when people are putting you down. And finally, you'll find out how to stand on your own two feet without stepping on other people's toes so you can avoid being hurt or causing hurt.

· Author's Note ·

My dad used to tell me, "Good ideas are a dime a dozen, and they're not worth a plug nickel if you don't act on them." I know these Tongue Fu! techniques can benefit you if you follow up and act on them.

You will be more likely to take action on your intentions if you consistently apply these ideas to your life. A favorite teacher used to say, "A short pencil is better than a long memory." Please read *Tongue Fu!* with pencil in hand (unless you are reading a copy from a library). Underline important points. Make notes to yourself in the margin. When you come across a suggestion that's particularly relevant or timely, write it on an index card and post it on your mirror or bulletin board. You've heard the saying "Out of sight, out of mind"? Do the opposite. If you keep your action plans in sight, you'll keep them in mind. Those constant visual reminders will help you use what you've learned.

CAN I QUOTE YOU ON THAT?

"The wisdom of the wise and the experience of the ages are perpetuated by quotations."
—BENJAMIN DISRAELI

Disraeli was right. Quotations appear throughout this book in the hopes you'll be able to apply these timeless observations to your daily situations. Whenever possible, I've given the author's name. But you'll notice that many of the quotes are attributed to that prolific pundit Anonymous. Some were contributed by workshop participants who didn't recall the source, some appear in quote books and weren't credited to a particular individual, and others scrolled across my computer's screen saver.

If you know the sources of any of the anonymous quotes, please contact me on the phone or on-line numbers in the back of this book. I would appreciate your assistance in helping me give credit where credit is due.

You'll also find many definitions in the text. Looking up a familiar word in the dictionary frequently yields a welcome, fresh perspective. I'm often delighted to discover a deeper understanding of the word's meaning and hope you find the elaborations enlightening.

LEARN FROM OTHERS

"We should learn from the mistakes of others. We don't have time to make them all ourselves." —GROUCHO MARX

I want to thank all the many workshop participants who so willingly provided me with the examples you'll find throughout this book. It's said that "a doctor is a shortcut to health; a coach is a shortcut to peak performance; a teacher is a shortcut to knowledge." These Tongue Fu! Coup contributors graciously agreed to share their stories so you could benefit from their experiences and save yourself trial-and-error learning. I hope their insights will be a shortcut to your success in dealing with difficult people.

Jawaharlal Nehru pointed out that "there is only one thing that remains to us, that cannot be taken away: to act with courage and dignity and to stick to the ideals that give meaning to your life." Ideal is defined as "a standard of . . . excellence . . . an ultimate object or aim of endeavor."

You may think Tongue Fu! is idealistic. It is, and it works. Thousands of Tongue Fu! graduates are proof that you can lead an infinitely more meaningful and rewarding life if you have the courage to treat discourteous people with dignity. Commit to living up to these ideals on a daily basis and you can ultimately improve the outcome of your every interaction at work, at home, and in your community.

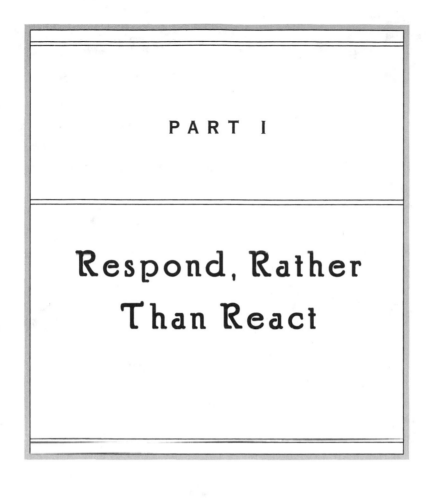

PART I

Respond, Rather Than React

· Chapter 1 ·

Fast-Forward Through Frustration

What do you do when someone says something unfair or unkind?

Do you remain silent because you don't know what to say? Do you speak up only to wish you hadn't? Or do you think of the perfect response on the way home?

It's natural to take offense if someone yells at you or blames you for something that's not your fault. You may think, "This isn't fair!" or "What a jerk!" or "I don't get paid enough to deal with this." These reactions, though understandable, only make matters worse. Why? Blurting out how you feel establishes an adversarial atmosphere and escalates negative emotions. In fact, going with your initial reaction almost always hurts more than it helps.

From now on, the goal is to think before you speak. This chapter offers several techniques to help you think on your feet so you won't automatically lash back when verbally attacked.

ASK YOURSELF: "HOW WOULD I FEEL?"

"All the mistakes I have made, all the follies I have witnessed, all the errors I have committed have been the result of action without thought."

—ANONYMOUS

How can you learn to act *with* thought? By understanding that if you're angry with someone, you're probably only seeing things from your point of view. To see things from the other person's point of view, use the Empathy Phrase "How would I feel?" "How would I feel if I were in their shoes?" "How would I feel if this was happening to me?" The power of this phrase is that it removes animosity by helping you experience the other person's side.

You may not like the other person's behavior, the Empathy Phrase can help you understand it. As Confucius said, "The more a man knows, the more he forgives." Taking the time to find out what's causing unpleasant behavior can be one step toward forgiving it.

TURN EXASPERATION INTO EMPATHY

"Empathy is one of the best indicators of maturity."
—TONGUE FU'ISM

A workshop participant wrote to report his success with the Empathy Phrase.

> My mother has been in a rest home for the last three years. I used to dread driving out to see her every Saturday because all she ever did was complain. She complained about her roommate. She complained that no one ever came to see her. She complained about her aches and pains.
>
> Then I asked myself, "How would I feel if I were in bed eighteen hours a day, seven days a week? How would I feel if I lived six feet away from someone I didn't even like, who played the TV so loud I could hardly hear myself think? How would I feel if days went by and none of my children had an hour to come and visit me? How would I feel if every morning I woke up, I hurt, and I couldn't see a day when that wasn't going to be the case?"

Asking "How would I feel?" moved me out of my selfish frustration. When I took the time to consider what my mom's days were like, and when I stopped to think of all she's done for me, I realized it's the least I can do to spend a couple hours with her and be more supportive.

If you don't like the way people are treating you, you have a choice. You can react without thinking and give them a piece of your mind, or you can take a second to see things from their perspective and give yourself peace of mind.

TAKE OFFENSE VS. TAKE PITY

"If we were to make the conscious and frequent effort of treating others with consideration, the effects on us and on society as a whole would be amazing.'
—HENRY CHARLES LINK

A reservations manager for a major hotel contributed her Tongue Fu! Coup at the follow-up meeting of our training. "Working the front desk can get frustrating sometimes because we're the first point of contact. That means we hear about everything' that's gone wrong. We hear about late flights, lost bags, standing in line for rental cars. We even hear complaints about the weather!

"The day after our session, a bedraggled couple showed up at the front desk early in the morning and wanted to register. I explained that check-in wasn't until three P.M., and that it would be several hours before their room would be available. The obviously exhausted young man lost it. 'What do you mean, we can't get our room? This is our honeymoon! We've been up for thirty-six hours straight. We're so tired we can hardly stand up.'

"I explained that we were 100 perent booked with a large convention and that the group wasn't expected to check out until after their closing luncheon. The newlywed threw a fit. He seemed to think if he hassled me loudly and long enough, I could somehow locate an empty suite for them. The more insistent he became, the more irritated I got.

"I was about to lose my temper when I remembered our workshop and realized I was only considering how I felt. When I asked myself, 'How would I feel if I was so exhausted I could hardly see straight and I was told I'd have to wait another six hours to get my room? How would I feel if Murphy's Law decided to turn my romantic honeymoon into a nightmare?'

"As soon as I experienced his side, I felt an outpouring of sympathy for him and his bride. A minute before he had been a pain in the neck; now I was able to forgive him because I empathized with his situation. I gave them a coupon for a complimentary breakfast buffet and arranged for them to use our hospitality suite so they could change into their bathing suits and nap on the beach. They came back later in the day and thanked me for being so helpful."

This hotel manager had found out for herself the value of Empathy Phrases. Instead of putting those difficult people in their place, she had put herself in their place and was able to respond with compassion rather than contempt.

ASK YOURSELF: "WHY ARE THEY BEING DIFFICULT?"

"The weak can never forgive. Forgiveness is the attribute of the strong."
—MAHATMA GANDHI

Would you like to know another question that can help you forgive and forget? Simply ask yourself: "Why are they being difficult?"

My son Andrew and I stopped by our local ice cream store to buy dessert for his birthday. The place was packed with people, ordering sundaes, milk shakes, or something complicated. A frazzled high school girl was the only one behind the counter. She was working as fast as she could, but the "hurrieder" she went, the "behinder" she got.

After thirty long minutes, she finally called our number. I handed her our slip and asked for three quarts of chocolate chip ice cream. This request was obviously the last straw for the overworked employee. Hands on hips, she said incredulously, "Three *quarts* of chocolate chip ice cream!?! Do you know how *hard* it is to get ice cream out of these containers?!"

If I hadn't been such a proponent of Tongue Fu!, I would have been tempted to let loose the rather uncharitable comment on the tip of my tongue, which was, "Well, excuuuse meeee! I thought this was an ice cream store." That sarcastic response wouldn't have made either of us feel any better. Instead, I held my tongue (Tongue Glue!) and asked myself: "Why would she say something like that?" Realizing how overwhelmed she probably felt, I inquired sympathetically, "Has it been that kind of day?"

Her hostility disappeared. She let out a huge sigh and said, "Oh, yes! I've been the only one here all day, and it's been nonstop since ten this morning. I was supposed to get off an hour ago, and the owner still hasn't come in." She continued to unburden herself while she packaged our ice cream. When we left, she gave us a big smile and a friendly wave. Such is the power of Tongue Fu! That question helped both of us regain a positive perspective.

HOW THESE TECHNIQUES BENEFIT YOU

"If you are patient in one moment of anger, you will escape a hundred days of sorrow."   —CHINESE PROVERB

The questions "How would I feel?" and "Why are they behaving this way?" can help you respond with sensitivity rather than sarcasm. Even if you're not sure what's behind someone's aggressive behavior, the few seconds it takes to wonder about his motivation can keep you from saying something you'll regret.

A workshop participant challenged this idea. "I don't agree. If someone gets on my nerves, they're going to hear about it! Why should I play peacemaker if the other person is the one who's out of line?"

This participant had introduced an issue that cartoonist Ashleigh Brilliant addresses in the caption to one of his cartoons: "Why should I be willing to compromise when I'm the one who's right?"

Indeed. Why *should* you invest the time and energy involved in finding out why someone is being unkind? Because it's to your benefit.

There have always been and always will be difficult people in the world. Virginia Satir suggested, "We must not allow other people's limited perceptions to define us." Conversely, we must not let *our* limited perceptions define other people. Impatience is often a by-product of ignorance. If you're about to snap back at someone who is testing your patience, remember that your contempt may be caused by limited knowledge of his situation. If you make someone pay for being unpleasant, *you're* going to pay right along with him. Using an Empathy Phrase is keeps you from getting in a bad mood and becoming involved in a no-win conflict.

WHAT IF THEY'RE WRONG?

"It is often better not to see an insult than to avenge it." —SENECA

Another skeptic added his opinion: "I'm not convinced. What if the ice cream shop employee isn't having a bad day? What if she's plain old incompetent? Am I supposed to ignore her poor service?"

Good point. If your attempts to turn bad service around fail, you have a choice. You may decide the person's actions are not worth avenging and opt to shrug it off and go on your way. Or you may decide you don't want to seem to support this bad behavior by overlooking it. If you choose to hold the person accountable for his actions, you can increase the likelihood of a satisfactory outcome by using these four steps to complain constructively.

> STEP 1. Resist the urge to tell off the impertinent employee. Any satisfaction you might get from reprimanding him would be short-lived. Your outburst would only reinforce his view that people are swine, would not motivate him to treat you better, and would ruin any chance of an amicable solution to the problem.

STEP 2. Inquire politely, "What is your name, please?" This simple phrase is often enough incentive for the employee to treat you with more courtesy. Why? He is no longer anonymous. He realizes he will be held responsible for his discourteous service.

STEP 3. State your Customer Rights and Wishes. "I have been a patron of this establishment for a long time, and I would like to continue giving you my business. Please speak to me with respect so I will want to come back."

STEP 4. If this effort to establish a more pleasant atmosphere doesn't work, then ask to see the supervisor. (If the manager is not available, request his/her name so you can follow up by phone or in writing.)

When the supervisor arrives, resist the urge to dump on the employee. If you yourself are rude when reporting rude behavior, the person in charge will be more likely to believe and back the employee. Report the incident in a gracious way and you can count on being taken seriously.

Remain calm and speak politely yet purposefully. "I know you take a lot of pride in your store, and I thought you might want to know the actions of this individual are compromising that." Explain what has happened and then appeal to the manager's interest in maintaining a good reputation. "I decided to bring this to your attention because it is inconsistent with the quality you stand for. What can be done about this?"

I have had to resort to complaining to management about an abrasive employee only a few times. Each time I've used a variation of this theme, and the supervisor has bent over backward to compensate for the staff member's regrettable behavior.

CHOOSE TO BE COMPASSIONATE

"We can be right, or we can be happy."

—*A COURSE IN MIRACLES*

Tongue Fu! is founded on the philosophy that not only is it possible, it's preferable to be charitable when someone's being cantankerous. Or as the Dalai Lama advised, "If you want *others* to be happy, practice compassion. If *you* want to be happy, practice compassion." If someone hurts you, that doesn't make it right to hurt them back. Doing so will only make both of you unhappy.

Goethe observed, "Treat people as if they were what they ought to be, and you help them become what they're capable of being." By choosing to respond to unpleasant people with empathy rather than irritation, you can often transform their hostility into harmony, circumvent anger, and make yourself and others happy in the process.

ACTION PLAN FOR
FAST-FORWARDING THROUGH FRUSTRATION

Imagine you're at a theater, standing in line for refreshments. The two employees behind the counter can't keep up with the demand. The movie is about to start, and it looks like you won't get your snacks in time to catch the beginning. You're not pleased with the slow service. How do you choose to respond?

WORDS TO LOSE	WORDS TO USE
You can be surly. *"Why doesn't management hire more employees? This is ridiculous."*	You can respond and be sympathetic. *"They're working as fast as they can. They're just understaffed."*
You can be impatient and exasperated. *"Why don't they hurry up? I've been waiting ten minutes."*	You can be understanding and empathetic. *"How would I feel if I was handling a crowd of this size?"*
You can blame them for their wrong behavior. *"You should have realized these were popular shows and scheduled more help."*	You can relax and choose to be compassionate. *You say with a friendly smile, "Could I please have two plain popcorns and a fruit punch?"*
You can continue to see things from only your point of view. *"This is lousy service. I'm never coming back here again. I didn't pay fifteen bucks to stand in line."*	You can put yourself in their place, fast-forward through your frustration, and forgive them. *"I can keep my peace of mind and rise above this petty incident. This isn't that big a deal."*

· Chapter 2 ·

Handle Hassles with Fun Fu!

Do you have a question you hate to be asked? Is there an event that fills you with anxiety?

Become a Fun Fu! (first cousin to Tongue Fu!) master. Develop a repertoire of ready responses so dreaded questions and situations no longer have the power to unnerve you.

This concept of Fun Fu! was perfectly demonstrated by a resourceful young man I "ran into" at the San Francisco Airport. I was riding a moving sidewalk down one of the long hallways when a commotion ahead caught my attention. A very tall man was coming toward me, and several people were pointing at him and giggling. I was taken aback by their terrible manners and thought they were being inexcusably rude.

As the individual moved closer, I could understand why they were amused. He was wearing a T-shirt with the inscirption, NO, I'M NOT A BASKETBALL PLAYER! As he passed by, I turned to say something and started laughing out loud. The back of his T-shirt read: ARE YOU A JOCKEY?

I had to meet this clever young man, so I jumped off the people mover and chased after him. I finally caught up with him and asked breathlessly, "Where did you get that terrific shirt?"

He grinned from ear to ear and said, "This is nothing. I have a whole drawer full at home. My favorite one says, 'I'm 6'13" and the weather up here is fine!' " He went on to explain: "I grew almost a foot between sixteen and eighteen. I didn't even want to leave the house because everywhere I went, people made smart-aleck remarks. My mom finally told me, 'If you can't beat 'em, join 'em.' She was the one who thought these up. Now I look forward to going out because I enjoy my height instead of being embarrassed by it."

How wise! If you have an attribute or condition that bothers you, doesn't it make sense to have fun *with* it instead of being frustrated *by* it?

WHAT ARE YOUR HOT BUTTONS?

"How come my parents can still push all my hot buttons?" "That's easy. They installed them." —GRAFFITI ON A WALL

Identify your hot buttons. What causes you to lose your temper or poise? Yogi Berra said, "Laughter is the shock absorber that eases the blows of life." Start collecting comebacks for those not-so-funny verbal jabs.

Wouldn't we like to have someone provide us with ready-made punch lines? When David Niven emceed the 1974 Academy Awards, the producer of the show anticipated an uninvited guest (it was the year of the streaker), so he created a quip—jest (!) in case. Sure enough, in the middle of the program a naked man raced across the stage and Niven was able to produce this seemingly off-the-cuff remark: "Just think. The only laugh that man will ever get is for showing off his . . . shortcomings." Bravo!

Since most of us can't rely on a professional joke writer to prepare our punch lines, we have to develop our own.

In every Tongue Fu! workshop, participants brainstorm Fun Fu! responses for their worst-nightmare scenarios. A successful career woman said she used to dread being asked what type of degree she had. "I didn't go to college, so that question always flustered me.

One time I was presenting a paper at an industry conference, and an audience member asked where I'd gone to school. I didn't know what to say at first. Then I spontaneously quipped that I had gone to UHK. The puzzled attendee asked, 'What's that?' I smiled and said, 'The University of Hard Knocks.' It got a chuckle, let me off the hook in a humorous way, and that's what I've been saying ever since."

A spry elderly gentleman admitted he resented being asked how old he was. "That offends me. My age is nobody's business but my own. Where do people get off asking such personal questions?" Our class put their heads together and came up with some tongue-in-cheek answers. Since the fellow was an active golfer, his favorite was "Let's just say I'm on the back nine."

A married couple in their mid-thirties said they had grown tired of being asked, "When are the two of you going to have children?" They liked someone's suggestion that they feign shock and exclaim, "We *knew* we forgot *something!*" They could also fend off too-personal questions with "Why do you ask?" That riposte is often enough to let people know you consider their inquiry off-limits.

SHOCKED VS. AMUSED

"Perhaps one has to be very old before one learns how to be amused rather than shocked."
—PEARL S. BUCK

The premise of Tongue Fu! is that it's important to learn *now* how to be amused rather than shocked if someone says something insensitive. There will *always* be people who make inappropriate remarks. Their barbs can't needle you unless you let them. Develop a mental thick skin.

I'll always remember the pain in a woman's voice when she asked, "What can I say when someone says, 'Wow, you've put on a lot of weight'? It really hurts my feelings when people comment, 'Packing on a few pounds, eh?' "

If what your tormentor says is true, you can acknowledge that with a "grin" of salt and say, "You're right!" and then change the subject. You can use self-deprecating humor and respond, "Yeah, I'm diet-impaired" or "I'm not fat, I'm just horizontally gifted." If the person is being deliberately cruel, you may choose to hold him accountable by noting, "Haven't we all?" The secret is not to buy into others' off-base remarks and not to give them an opportunity to follow up the first comment with a second. Simply respond with poise and then move the conversation to something else.

A woman who was still heavy several months after the delivery of her second child reported that she often ran into people who made such tactless comments as "I thought you already had your baby" or "Are you going to have another one?" Instead of being tongue-tied by their tactless observations, she pats her tummy while waggling her eyebrows à la Groucho Marx and retorts, "These are leftovers," and then switches the topic.

During a training session I conducted for the IRS, an auditor explained how he and his coworkers use Fun Fu! to counteract boorish behavior. "Just about everyone who walks in our door is antagonistic. They see us as the enemy, and they don't want to be here. Instead of being offended by this undeserved animosity (we're people too!), we've filled a bulletin board with comic strips that poke fun at the IRS, or Income Removal Service. One pictures an auditor telling a citizen, 'The secret is to stop thinking of it as *your* money.' These cartoons let the public know we're human. When taxpayers read these jokes and our sign that says, 'Sorry, we're IN!' their whole attitude changes—for the better."

You're never too old or too young to learn the power of laughter. With a last name like Horn, our two boys got a lot of teasing at school. It used to embarrass them to be called "horny" by their classmates. We knew if we could just come up with a Fun Fu! response, the verbal jabs would stop. Sure enough, after much brainstorming, Tom and Andrew found the perfect comeback. Their response: "That's our name. *Please* wear it out!" has made this a nonissue. If you have a characteristic that embarrasses you, enlist the help of friends to search for just the right thing to say, and you can turn misery into mirth.

NO COMMENT

"A closed mouth gathers no feet."   —TONGUE FU'ISM

Don't dignify truly outrageous accusations (e.g., the infamous "When did you stop beating your wife?") with any answer at all. Why? Bob Monkhouse explained it best: "Silence is not only golden, it's seldom misquoted." Don't even say, "I'm not going to answer that." If you take the bait, they'll have successfully hooked you with their taunt.

Instead, redirect the remark to a related topic. A famous film star did a masterful job of this one evening on a late-night television talk show. The host made a rather unkind observation about her film career. "All your movies have portrayed you as a sex kitten, haven't they?"

You could tell the actress was distressed by this sweeping categorization and didn't want to waste her fifteen minutes in the spotlight discussing this stereotype. She turned to the emcee, and instead of arguing with (and reinforcing) his characterization of her movie roles, she brightly asked, "Speaking of movies, would you like to see a clip from my new one?" Without causing her host to lose face, she adroitly picked up on part of his comment and moved on to a more constructive topic.

LEARN TO LAUGH AT LIFE

"I learned quickly that when I made others laugh, they liked me. This lesson I will never forget."   —ART BUCHWALD

Jim Pelley, a friend and professional speaker from Northern California, is a Fun Fu! black belt. He travels around the country presenting programs about humor in the workplace for Fortune 500 companies, and takes subscribers from ha-ha to aha in his funny and informative newsletter *Laughter Works.* Jim has given me permission to tell his signature story about a flight attendant who laughs at life and helps others do the same.

Jim describes the time he was seated next to The Original Difficult Person on a completely full coast-to-coast flight. This unhappy fellow complained about everything: his carry-on bag wouldn't fit in the overhead bin; he was squeezed into the middle seat of the middle row; it took almost two hours to serve lunch; and—the final insult—lunch was a light snack instead of a hot meal. Mr. Difficult took one bite of his sandwich, dropped it back on his plate, and angrily pushed the call button.

The flight attendant quickly appeared and asked politely, "Yes, sir, how may I help you?" He shoved the sandwich up toward her face and growled, "This sandwich is bad!"

The flight attendant looked from him to the sandwich.

She looked back at him and then stared at the sandwich.

She focused on him one more time, then shook her finger at the snack and scolded, *"Bad* sandwich, *bad* sandwich!"

The man jerked straight up in his seat. Jim said he couldn't help himself—he burst out laughing. After a moment of stunned silence, the disgruntled passenger started laughing too, and was quiet and cooperative from then on.

Jim approached the flight attendant later in the galley to congratulate her. "That was classic. Did you just think of that?" She replied, "I've been flying for twenty-five years. I discovered a long time ago I better learn how to handle difficult people because there's at least one on every flight. Unless I figured out how to turn them around, they were going to end up making me and everyone else on the plane miserable.

"I talked with other stews—that's what we called ourselves in those days—and asked how they handled challenging situations. What can we do when we're seventeenth in line and everyone's going to miss their connections? What can we say when we have a mechanical problem and have to return to the gate? I collected a variety of amusing comments so I can handle just about anything that happens."

She continued, "I've pledged to keep a sense of humor, no matter what! I decided that no one—regardless of how outrageous his behavior—was going to ruin my trip. You have no idea how many times that has saved me."

As Mark Twain said, "Humor is the great thing, the saving thing, after all. The minute it crops up, our irritations and resentments flit away, and a sunny spirit takes their place." Can you make a commitment to keep your sense of humor no matter what? It can enable you to handle challenges with a chuckle instead of a curse.

LIVE LIGHTLY

"It better befits a man to laugh at life than to lament over it."

—SENECA

I was checking out of a hotel at the end of a National Speakers Association convention and was fortunate to be standing next to Bob Murphy, former state senator from Nacogdoches, Texas, and one of the funniest men I've ever had the privilege to know. A bellhop walked by pushing a luggage cart with a large potted plant on it. Bob watched it roll by and then drawled, "I guess a dog must have ordered room service." After everyone in the vicinity quit guffawing, I asked Bob, "How do you come up with such funny lines?" He replied, "You've got to look at the world with smiling eyes."

From now on, stay alert for humorous asides. Mel Brooks was right when he observed, "Life literally abounds in comedy if you just look around you." If someone heckles *Tonight* show host Jay Leno and he fires back an inspired retort, remember it (and give him credit). If you're watching the Comedy Channel on TV or reading a newspaper and a joke makes you laugh out loud, write it down (and note the source). If you make a mistake, remember that to err is *humor* and rib yourself. By looking for laughs in all the right places, you can respond to stressful situations with equanimity rather than irritation.

If you would like more information on how to handle hassles with Fun Fu!, buy and study "jollytologist" Allen Klein's book *The Healing Power of Humor: Techniques for Getting Through Loss, Setbacks, Upsets, Disappointments, Difficulties, Trials, Tribulations, and All That Not-So-Funny Stuff.* (Whew!) This excellent reference features dozens of ways to use what Klein calls joke-jitsu to turn any disadvantage into an advantage. It is full of ways to help you look at life with smiling eyes.

ACTION PLAN FOR HANDLING
HASSLES WITH FUN FU!

You're unemployed and looking for work. After several months of answering ads and sweating through interviews, you finally have two good prospects, but they're not official yet. If one more person innocently asks, "How's the job search going?" you're not sure you can be held accountable for your behavior. How do you respond?

WORDS TO LOSE	WORDS TO USE
You let people push your hot buttons. *"If one more person asks me if I have a job yet, I'm going to explode."*	You can prepare responses to dreaded questions. *"Well, someone offered me a job selling* NO SOLICITING *signs door to door, but I turned them down."*
You can be frustrated by misfortune and regard it as an albatross. *"I'm never going to find work. I've invested hundreds of hours and I don't have anything to show for it."*	You can make fun of misfortune. *"I hadn't planned to retire quite this early. The good part is, I have weekdays free and I get to help coach my son's swim team."*
You can curse life and let people annoy you. *"What does he mean, am I running out of money?"*	You can keep your sense of humor, no matter what. *"I can't be out of money. I still have checks."* —Gracie Allen
You can resent thoughtless questions and be irritated by insensitive remarks. *"How am I supposed to respond to a stupid question like that? Doesn't he realize if I had found a job, I would have told him about it?"*	You can collect quips from the pros and use them to look at the world with smiling eyes. *"I walked by a business today that had two signs in the window,* EMPLOYEES WANTED *and* SELF-SERVICE. *So I went in and hired myself."* —Steven Wright

· Chapter 3 ·

Talk People Through Their Troubles

What do you do if an unhappy person starts pouring out his soul? Do you try to comfort him?

What you may not realize is that such well-intentioned words as "It can't be *that* bad" or "Come on, look at the bright side" invalidate rather than encourage someone who is feeling sad. Attempts to reason—"You can't expect to do it perfectly the first time" or "You'll feel better tomorrow"—only rankle. When people are troubled, they want sympathy, not solutions.

USE THE THERAPIST'S TOOL

"No one wants advice—only corroboration."   —JOHN STEINBECK

Next time you're concerned about someone, use the Therapist's Tool to talk her *through* her problems rather than trying to talk her *out* of them.

What is the Therapist's Tool? It involves paraphrasing back what someone has said in an effort to confirm, clarify, and pursue her train of thought. Therapists don't indicate whether they agree with what's being said; they simply repeat it with upward inflection.

If a patient tells a therapist, "I don't have any friends," a therapist wouldn't reply, "Surely you have at least *one* friend." Instead of making the patient feel less isolated, that well-meaning reality check would come across as a rebuke, further evidence that no one really understands.

A therapist tries to help patients explore how they feel. Therapists accomplish this by mirroring what's being said rather than by minimizing it. In the case of our lonely patient, the therapist might respond: "You feel like you don't have any friends?"

The client would elaborate: "Yeah, I work in an office with over a hundred people and no one even talks to me unless it's about business. It's like I'm a nonperson."

Once again, rather than interjecting a reaction or recommendation, a therapist would just restate what has been said. "So, the people at your job don't pay much attention to you?"

"Yeah, if you're not a member of the in crowd, it's like you don't exist." The patient would then continue the catharsis of his feelings of rejection and loneliness.

The word *catharsis* means "a . . . purgation that brings about spiritual renewal or release from tension." It is also "elimination of a complex [fear or panic] by bringing it to consciousness and affording it expression." By paraphrasing what patients say *without* trying to cheer them up or solve their problems, therapists help clients become conscious of what is bothering them. By purging his psychic pain to a sympathetic ear, the patient can release pent-up tension and then will be ready for corrective action.

REFLECT, DON'T REFUTE

"It is a luxury to be understood."　　　—RALPH WALDO EMERSON

Our son Andrew, who had just been fitted with prescription glasses, provided me with an opportunity to practice the Therapist's Tool.

Tears in his eyes, he trudged out of the optometrist's office and announced, "I look like a geek!"

I wanted to say, "You don't either. You look fine." However, those words meant to console him would have contradicted him.

Rather than trying to reassure him, I simply reflected what he'd said: "You don't like the way your new glasses look?" He wailed, "All the kids at school are going to laugh at me."

BTF (Before Tongue Fu!) I might have tried to soothe him. "Andrew, don't be silly. Your classmates probably won't even notice you're wearing glasses." My attempt to be objective would only have alienated him. My efforts to support him would have shut him down. Instead I paraphrased what he had said: "You're afraid your classmates are going to tease you about your glasses?"

"Yeah. Why do I have to wear these ugly things, anyway?"

My first impulse was to say rationally, "You need them to see better." However, emotion is irrational and doesn't respond to logic. Any attempt to explain why he had to wear glasses would have produced irritation, not enlightenment. Rather than trying to reason with him, I articulated his *wishes:* "So you wish you didn't have to wear glasses?"

"Yeah." He sighed and continued to work through his feelings.

When we got home, Andrew impulsively gave me a hug and said, "Thanks, Mom." I asked, "What for?" He shrugged and said, "You know." I think what he was saying was "Thank you for listening and not lecturing. Thank you for talking *with* me, not *at* me."

PARAPHRASE VS. PARROT

"You can't reason someone out of something they weren't reasoned into."
—JONATHAN SWIFT

Barbara, one of my workshop participants, took exception to the idea of reflecting. "If one of my staff members dumps a problem in my lap and I repeat it word for word, they'd look at me like I was crazy and exclaim, 'That's what I just said!'"

Barbara had just pointed out why it's important to paraphrase rather than parrot. Parroting what someone's just said, repeating it word for word, is not recommended because such speech seems condescending or patronizing. Paraphrasing is using your *own* words to summarize the essence of what someone has said. This sincere effort to ensure an exchange of meaning won't offend people, it will delight them. It means you care enough to get what they're saying right.

Barbara had also provided me with the perfect opportunity to introduce this important proverb: "Rules make good servants and poor masters."

I said, "The Therapist's Tool (and the other techniques in this book) are servants, not masters. They are not universal panaceas, guaranteed to work every time with everyone. It is unrealistic to speak in absolutes."

Please think of *Tongue Fu!* as a banquet of ideas. Take from it what's appropriate for each situation. If you're waiting on ten people, you may not have the time or interest to talk each one through his or her troubles. If you don't have a relationship with someone, you may not care enough to help her unburden her concerns. The techniques outlined in Chapter 4, "End Complaints Instantly," will help you deal with such scenarios.

BE A SOUNDING BOARD, NOT A SCOLDING BOARD

"We want people to feel with us more than to act for us."
—GEORGE ELIOT

The next time people close to you are unhappy, remember you can't argue anxiety away. Patiently feed back what they're feeling instead of trying to fast-forward them through their angst. Elicit from them what they want to happen instead of explaining why they have to do something they don't want to do, which will only increase their resistance.

A woman was thoughtful enough to report her success with this idea. "My daughter came home from her first soccer practice and announced she wanted to quit the team. I was stunned because soccer is her favorite sport. She's been looking forward to it ever since last season. I was about to say, 'You can't mean that!' when I remembered the story about your son.

"Instead of telling her she was being ridiculous, I asked, 'So you didn't have a good time at soccer practice?' and it all came out. She was upset because the coach had switched her to a defensive position. She scored a lot of goals last year and was counting on being a forward. I was about to explain that soccer is a team sport and everyone can't always play the position they want . . . when I remembered what you said about troubled people wanting to feel heard, not hassled.

"I resisted the temptation to mouth those platitudes and just kept reflecting what she said. Instead of blathering about the reasons behind her coach's decision and how she should be mature about it, I said, 'So you wish you could play your old position?' She regained perspective after purging her feelings, and like your son, gave me a hug and a thank you for helping her talk things through."

Remember, unhappy people want to get things off their chest, not be beat over the head with what they should do or feel. By reflecting what they're saying rather than refuting it, you can help them unburden what's bothering them. They'll feel better and thank you for being that rarest of individuals, an empathetic listener.

ACTION PLAN FOR TALKING
PEOPLE THROUGH THEIR TROUBLES

You brought your newborn son home a couple of weeks ago, and your daughter is growing increasingly resentful of her baby brother's demands. One day when you tell her you don't have time right now to read a story, she breaks into tears and sobs, "You love Brian more than me!" How do you deal with this?

WORDS TO LOSE	WORDS TO USE
You hasten to reassure her, and she feels she's said something wrong. *"Sissie, that's not true, and you know it."*	You reflect what she's said so she feels heard. *"You feel we love Brian more than you?"*
You try to comfort her and she feels contradicted. *"Don't be silly, I do too spend time with you. Didn't we go to the park yesterday?"*	You paraphrase her comments to help her talk things through. *"So it seems I don't spend much time with you anymore?"*
You try to reason with her and she gets annoyed. *"Babies need a lot of attention because they can't take care of themselves."*	You express her wishes instead of trying to explain things. *"So you wish we could spend more time together like we used to?"*
You tell her what she should feel and she feels unheard. *"You have to understand I can't drop everything to play with you whenever you want."*	You articulate what she wants and she feels understood. *"So you want me to put some time aside so we can read your favorite book?"*

· Chapter 4 ·

End Complaints Instantly

What do you do if someone complains? Do you explain why they didn't get what they wanted when they wanted it? This is a common response. Unfortunately, it usually makes the complainer feel *more* aggravated rather than less. Why? Explanations come across as excuses. The complainer will get even more exasperated because he'll feel you're not being accountable.

Imagine you're at work and the telephone rings. No sooner do you pick it up than the caller launches into a complaint: "What kind of business are you running, anyway? I requested a catalog from you three weeks ago and I *still* haven't received it. What's taking so long?"

Understand that the caller doesn't really want to know why it's taking so long. If you say, "Several employees have been out sick with the flu and we've gotten behind on our paperwork," the customer will perceive your reasons as rationalizations. He may snap back, "I don't want to hear your office health history. All I want to know is are you or aren't you going to send me that catalog?"

WHEN PEOPLE COMPLAIN, DON'T EXPLAIN

"There is no waste of time like making explanations."
—BENJAMIN DISRAELI

From this day forward when people complain, ask yourself if what they are saying is basically true. If it is, say these magic words: "You're right!"

Usually, when people are upset, they have a legitimate reason to be so. Instead of outlining what went wrong, acknowledge what they've said and move on to what can be done about it. Explanations extend arguments, agreeing ends them.

I developed a rhyme to help a group of employees remember this concept: "When people complain, if we explain, it will be in vain." A few picked up on my rhythm and said, "When customers complain, if we explain, it will only cause pain." A musically inclined participant added, "When customers complain, don't explain, take the AAA Train."

AGREE, APOLOGIZE, ACT

"Every great mistake has a halfway moment, a split second when it can be recalled and perhaps remedied."
—PEARL S. BUCK

Recently I witnessed what happens when an employee takes the AAA Train with a complainer. I arrived at my doctor's office for an appointment and found all the seats in the reception area taken except for one chair, which I promptly claimed. An hour later, we were all still waiting, and the man across from me was *not* a happy camper. He thumbed restlessly through the pile of tattered, outdated magazines and squirmed in his chair, impatiently jiggling his foot up and down and agitatedly checking his watch every few minutes. He finally marched over to the receptionist's window and rapped sharply on the glass.

The medical assistant opened the panel and asked politely, "Yes, sir, how may I help you?"

He demanded, "What is going on? I had a three P.M. appointment. It's four o'clock, and I still haven't seen the doctor."

Instead of explaining what had gone wrong (which would only have further annoyed the irate individual), the receptionist took the AAA Train.

- **Agree:** "You're right, sir. You did have a three o'clock appointment . . ."

- **Apologize:** ". . . and I'm sorry you've had to wait so long. The doctor has been held up in surgery."

- **Act:** "Let me call the hospital and ask the nurse how much longer he's going to be. Thank you for understanding. I appreciate your being so patient."

As you can imagine, the gentleman stopped taking his frustration out on the employee. What else could he do in the face of such gracious efficiency?

EXPEDITE COMPLAINTS

"It takes less time to do something right than to explain why it was done wrong."
—HENRY WADSWORTH LONGFELLOW

From this day forward, don't make an excuse, make an effort. Instead of taking the time to tell someone why things went wrong, use that time to start making it right!

A man laughed ruefully when I introduced this idea. He said, "I wish I'd known this last Friday. I was supposed to pick my wife up after work to go to dinner. I left my office on time, but the drive took three times longer than it should have because I got stuck in a traffic jam. A block away from her building, I could see her pacing back and forth on the curb and could tell she was fuming.

"When I pulled up, she yanked open the car door and shouted, 'Where have you been? You were supposed to be here at five-thirty!'

"I didn't know any better then, so I tried to explain. 'It's not my fault. I've been sitting on the freeway all this time.'

"She stormed back, 'How was I supposed to know that? I was worried sick that you had forgotten or that something had happened to you.'

"I said it wasn't fair to blame me. We argued back and forth until I finally blew up and told her to get off my case. That disagreement ruined what was supposed to have been an enjoyable evening. I realize now I could have prevented this whole unfortunate incident if I'd just used the Three As and said, 'You're right. I was supposed to be here at five-thirty, and I'm sorry you had to wait. An accident caused gridlock on the highway. From now on, if I'm going to pick you up, I'll leave early so if traffic is bad I can still be on time.' "

WHAT IF IT'S NOT YOUR FAULT?

"Most people spend more time and energy going around problems than in trying to solve them."
—HENRY FORD

A Department of Motor Vehicles employee didn't like what he was hearing. "Why should we apologize for something that's not our fault? Yesterday a guy couldn't renew his driver's license because he didn't have his insurance papers with him, and he got upset at *me* because he was going to have to start the process all over. I couldn't believe it. How could he blame me when there's a big sign out front that lists all the needed documents? I'm not about to say I'm sorry; *he's* the one who didn't read the instructions."

I said to the DMV employee, "It's not that you have to apologize, it's just that it's to your advantage to at least acknowledge his frustration. If you tell the customer what he already knows—'Hey, it's not *my* fault you didn't bring the right forms!'—he's going to become even angrier, which is just going to make your day more stressful.

"Suppose you say, 'I know it's frustrating to find out you don't have the proper paperwork. If you'll fill out this application now, I can save it until tomorrow. If you can come back with your insurance papers between two and three in the afternoon, the slowest part of the day for us, all we have to do is verify them and you'll be set.' "

I asked the DMV staffer, "How would the customer respond if you chose to help him out this way?" The guy replied, "He'd probably stop yelling at me." Exactly!

In case after case, the class saw that taking the AAA Train works to their advantage. James Matthew Barrie observed, "Those who bring sunshine to the lives of others cannot keep it from themselves." Participants realized that telling someone they're sorry about what happened doesn't mean they're admitting guilt, it's just a way of commiserating so that the person feels someone cares about their plight. The class concluded that if the attitude they project is "It's your problem, not mine," the upset individual will make it their problem!

I was presenting this idea in a Tongue Fu! workshop for the city/county emergency medical service department, and one of the paramedics disagreed with me. "Our supervisor told us that we should never apologize for anything because it means we're responsible. Yesterday our ambulance crew wasn't able to save a drowning victim and the bereaved spouse said it was our fault. There's no way I was going to agree and give her the impression she was right."

He had a point. If someone is complaining and she has the facts wrong, you have to ask yourself if correcting her will serve any purpose. Many times the facts are beside the point. Arguing back and forth about who's to blame won't undo what happened. In cases where it's not appropriate to agree with a complainant, at least acknowledge her emotions and take helpful action. Instead of saying, "There was nothing we could do. He was gone by the time we got here," the paramedic could have taken the Express AA Train and dealt with the widow's grief more tactfully:

- **Acknowledge:** "Mrs. Palmer, I'm so sorry about your loss."

- **Act:** "How can I help? Is there a family member I can call for you?"

RESOLVE VS. THE RUNAROUND

"Don't make excuses—make good."   —FRANK HUBBARD

Taking the Express AA Train (Acknowledge, Act) immediately defuses a complainer's emotional time bomb and prevents the situation from becoming explosive. By focusing on what can be done now instead of what should have been done and wasn't, you can often remedy a mistake before it gets blown out of proportion.

I was able to use this idea myself recently. We were having friends over for dinner Saturday night and I had agreed to stay home and get things ready. My husband walked in at five-thirty after a hard day at the observatory. He took one look at the chaos and exclaimed, "Sam, this house is a mess."

If I hadn't just given a Tongue Fu! workshop the day before, I might have forgotten myself and tried to explain: "Oh, I know it's a mess, but the neighborhood kids have been over all day. The phone hasn't stopped ringing, and I had to go out for some errands . . ."

Those excuses wouldn't have helped. Instead, I looked at him and said, "You're right, the house is a mess . . . and if you'll grab a broom and start sweeping, I know we can have it ready by the time Dianne and Gerald get here."

Situation resolved.

THANK(?!) PEOPLE FOR COMPLAINING

"The mark of a successful organization isn't whether or not it has problems, it's whether it has the same problems it had last year."
                    —JOHN FOSTER DULLES

A grocery store manager contributed this thought-provoking insight, "I heard supermarket magnate Stu Leonard say at a conference, 'A customer who complains is my best friend.' That one simple statement changed my whole approach to handling criticism. I used to dread complaints, but now I welcome them. Mr.

Leonard helped me see that if people aren't bringing problems to me, it doesn't mean things are perfect. It just means we're not hearing about our mistakes, which means we're not correcting them, which means we're losing business. I would rather know when someone is dissatisfied so I have a chance to turn them around. Customers are accustomed to getting the runaround when something goes wrong. When we thank them for complaining, they are disarmed and impressed. Our goal is to make every customer a repeat customer. This policy helps accomplish that."

Great idea. Remember the story at the beginning of this chapter about the customer who hadn't received her catalog? Imagine the goodwill the employee could generate if instead of going on and on about why the brochure hadn't been sent, he took the AAA Train and let the woman know how much he appreciated her reporting this oversight so he could correct it.

- **Agree:** "You're right, Mrs. Hughes. You did request that catalog several weeks ago . . ."

- **Apologize:** ". . . and I'm sorry you haven't received it yet."

- **Act:** "If I could please have your name and address again, I'll personally make up the packet and send it out in today's mail."

- **Appreciate:** "We appreciate you bringing this to our attention. We're glad you're interested in our products, and we want to make sure you receive that information promptly. Thanks for taking the time to call."

My favorite quote about service comes from Michael LeBouef's book *How to Win Customers and Keep Them for Life:* "There's not a lot of traffic on the extra mile." The employee's extra effort could make the difference in whether Mrs. Hughes chooses to make a purchase. Taking the (cross-country?) AAAA Train would exceed the customer's expectations and create a sense of trust: "You can count on us to keep our promises."

The White House Office of Consumer Affairs found that if you handle complaints well, people will feel better about you than if nothing had gone wrong in the first place. From this day forward, when someone complains, don't explain, use your brain. Take the AA, AAA, or AAAA Train, and it will be to your gain.

ACTION PLAN FOR ENDING
COMPLAINTS INSTANTLY

Imagine you're a food server at a restaurant. In the middle of a busy evening, a guest calls you over to his table, points to his entree, and says, "Waiter, I ordered the special because it was supposed to be fresh. This salmon tastes frozen to me. I think it's been a long time since this fish has seen any water." What do you do?

WORDS TO LOSE	WORDS TO USE
You can tell them what went wrong and why. *"We were supposed to have fresh salmon tonight, but the fish market ran out, so we substituted fresh frozen."*	You can ask yourself if what he is saying is basically true, and if so, agree with it. *"You're right, sir, the menu does say the salmon is fresh . . ."*
You can belabor an explanation and extend the argument. *"The chef told us it was supposed to be just as good. He tasted it and said he couldn't tell the difference."*	You can apologize and take action to end the argument before it begins. *. . . and I'm sorry you didn't get what you requested. I'd be glad to replace it with another entree of your choice."*
You can refuse to take responsibility for something that's not your fault. *"It wasn't my decision. They should have taken it off the menu."*	You can thank them for bringing this to your attention and take the AAAA Train. *"I appreciate you telling me this. We want to make sure you enjoy your meal and choose to come back."*

· Chapter 5 ·

Gracefully Exit Arguments

What can you do if you become involved in a no-win discussion?

It's obvious you are never going to change their mind, and they are never going to change yours. If you continue on this cerebral cul-de-sac, you could end up hurting each other's feelings and saying something that irreparably harms your relationship.

A Russian proverb states, "Once a word is spoken it flies, you can't catch it." The purpose of this chapter is to help you learn how to catch angry words *before* they fly out of your mouth. You will discover several ways to politely escape an argument so you both can avoid saying something you regret.

DISAGREE WITHOUT BEING DISAGREEABLE

"Part of the happiness of life consists not in fighting battles but in avoiding them. A masterly retreat is in itself a victory."

—NORMAN VINCENT PEALE

An effective way to sidestep stalemates is to observe, "We're both right" and to then segue to a safer topic.

In almost every controversey, each person has legitimate points. It's not that one is true and the other is false, that one is good and the other is bad. Both "sides" have valid views. Instead of seeing each other as mortal enemies, understand you simply have opposite opinions about an emotional issue.

A workshop participant said he wished he'd known this technique the preceding weekend. "My wife and I went to her parents' house Sunday night for supper. During dinner I mentioned that the freeway construction was stalled again. What a mistake! My father-in-law said he was glad. 'That freeway never should have been built in the first place! It's devastating an important historical valley.'

"Well, I spend over an hour each way commuting to work, five days a week. I told him I thought the highway was a necessary evil because there are four times as many cars as there were ten years ago, on the same number of roads. My wife's dad grumbled that it was typical of my selfish generation to think more about our commute time than a significant archeological site.

"I lost my patience and told him, 'You can't stop progress.' That did it. My father-in-law threw down his napkin and stood up and walked away, saying, 'I don't have to sit here and listen to this at my own dinner table.'

"I wish the whole thing had never happened. If I had been more alert to how volatile this subject was for him, I could have prevented the whole unfortunate incident by saying, 'Let's agree to disagree about this,' and politely steered the conversation to something else."

He was correct. As George Bernard Shaw observed, "There is no accomplishment so easy to acquire as politeness, and none more profitable."

HELP BOTH PARTIES SAVE FACE

"Good manners are made up of petty sacrifices."
—RALPH WALDO EMERSON

Imagine you and your partner disagree about how to discipline your teenager, who is misbehaving. You feel your partner is too punitive. He thinks you're too permissive. Your discussion about this issue escalates into a family feud.

Your mate says, "He's never going to respect us if we don't start showing him who's running this household." You say, "He's going to become even more rebellious if we ground him." Your partner argues, "It's our home. If he wants to live here, he has to abide by our rules." You counter with "he's seventeen, almost an adult. You can't treat him like a child." And so on.

Use the five words "We're on the same side" to regain perspective before you become the house divided against itself. That one sentence can help you work side *by* side instead of side *against* side.

Sam Levenson said, "We may not always see eye to eye. We can try to see heart to heart." In other words, just because you don't agree doesn't mean you have to be enemies. Saying "Hey, we both want the same thing" can help you remember you both have the same destination, just different ways of getting there. These phrases get you out of an adversarial mode and guide you back into working cooperatively to resolve a shared concern.

A woman said resignedly, "These techniques are nice, but they won't work with my husband. He's got to win every argument."

If you share this woman's dilemma, don't worry. We'll discuss in detail how you can tactfully terminate one-sided conversations later in the book. In fact, there's a whole chapter dedicated to this topic because it's such a universal dilemma.

DISENGAGE FROM DEAD-END DISCUSSIONS WITH DIGNITY

"I never saw an instance of one or two disputants convincing the other by argument."
—THOMAS JEFFERSON

What if you're negotiating a contract and you've reached an impasse? The other side isn't willing to budge, and neither are you. If you press this point, you could sacrifice all that you have accomplished.

Say, "Let's come back to this one," and then move on to a less controversial aspect of the agreement. This phrase is the key to changing the subject without having to change your mind. Later on, when you have reestablished an amicable atmosphere, return to the stumbling block and tackle it under more favorable circumstances.

I was lunching with several colleagues and the conversation turned to the governor's race. The campaign had turned ugly, with each party charging the other with dirty deeds. My companions were on opposite sides of the political fence, and their discussion became heated. One turned to me and asked, "Who do you think should be elected governor?" I wasn't about to get involved in their no-win debate. I put my hands up and said with a smile, "Leave me out of this one."

REVERSING VS. RECONCILING POSITIONS

"The overall purpose of human communication is—or should be— reconciliation."
                                                    —M. SCOTT PECK

"To think is to differ," noted Clarence Darrow. Yet people who think differently often become attached to their positions and don't want to reverse themselves. They dig in their heels and persist to resist. The phrases in this chapter and others such as "different strokes for different folks" and "six of one, half-dozen of another" are all gentle ways to give participants a face-saving out so they can detour a dispute.

A fellow trainer and I had the privilege of attending a seminar given by a revered management visionary (then in his eighties). It became apparent as the program progressed that this brilliant pioneer was slipping in and out of his full mental faculties. One moment he would be lucid and articulate, the next he would ramble on about a completely unrelated subject.

At one point, he took a firm stance that was the exact opposite of the position he had taken earlier. An audience member brought this reversal to his attention. Our speaker vehemently denied he had made the original statement and took umbrage that this attendee had had the audacity to challenge him. The participant, convinced he was right, persevered.

My friend, an expert on negotiation, could tell this test of wills wasn't going to serve anyone in the room. Neither person intended to back down, and their clash could continue ad infinitum to no avail. So he stood up and in a courteous yet firm voice said, "You're both right." He went on to give examples supporting each viewpoint and then asked a leading question about the next step on the handout to graciously and subtly get the speaker back on course.

MALE VS. FEMALE STYLES

"We mistakenly believe that if our partners love us, they will act and behave in certain ways—the ways we react and behave when we love someone."
—JOHN GRAY

In *Men Are from Mars, Women Are from Venus* and *You Just Don't Understand,* John Gray and Deborah Tannen have done an excellent job of explaining why couples end up arguing. Because men and women have different communication styles, they often misinterpret what the other is saying. A man may take his wife's claim that she's unhappy personally instead of realizing she's just letting off steam. The woman may resent her husband's well-meaning attempts to offer advice when all she wants is a sympathetic shoulder. Despite loving intentions, these breakdowns in communication result in hurt-filled conflicts.

The good news is that even though men and women operate on different frequencies, they can learn to communicate on the same wavelength. Women can learn that grumbling is good (Gray points out that it means the man is considering the woman's request versus his needs), and men can learn that when a woman talks about her troubles, she doesn't necessarily want her guy to fix it. If you're in a relationship, buy these books. Reading them and applying their insights can help you and your partner maintain your marital magic.

CULTURAL DIFFERENCES MEAN COMMUNICATION DIFFERENCES

"England and America are two countries separated by the same language."
—GEORGE BERNARD SHAW

A fellow professional speaker who is an expert on international protocol said to be sure to mention how important it is to honor cultural customs. After giving hundreds of training programs on diversity, Sondra is still shocked at how little Americans know about what is appropriate when dealing with people from other countries. "Before traveling abroad, for business or for pleasure, take the time to study the country's etiquette so you don't unintentionally offend residents by violating their cultural norms."

Sondra added, "Be sensitive to the different ethnic groups in your company or community. Many arguments arise because people naively assume their way of doing things is the only way and the right way. A supervisor in one of the companies I consult with didn't hire a talented college graduate because the young woman kept her face averted during the entire interview. 'She wouldn't even look me in the eye,' he grumped. 'How could I trust her?' he wrongly concluded. What he didn't know was that juniors in some Asian cultures are taught to defer to seniors and show their respect by lowering their eyes."

As Shaw observed, sharing the same language doesn't guarantee you share the same interpretation of what is being said or done. Realize that people are different, and different is not wrong.

From now on don't let differences turn into disagreements. Exit arguments with "save face" phrases, and remember that you don't have to be enemies just because you don't see things eye to eye.

ACTION PLAN FOR GRACEFULLY EXITING ARGUMENTS

You have reserved the neighborhood park for your parents' fiftieth wedding anniversary. You're setting up the picnic tables and streamers when another family shows up and insists they reserved the park for their son's graduation party. They accuse you of taking over the pavilion and threaten to call security to escort you off the property. What do you do?

WORDS TO LOSE	WORDS TO USE
You get drawn into the debate. *"Hold on a minute. We have as much right to the park as you do."*	You avoid a debate. *"I know we can work something out."*
You establish an adversarial atmosphere and escalate the argument. *"You should have gotten here earlier if you wanted these tables."*	You establish an agreeable atmosphere and escape from the argument. *"Let's see if we can arrange to get some extra tables set up."*
You use *you* words, which angers them even more. *"If you think you can just barge in and move us out, you're wrong."*	You use *we* words to avoid an impasse. *"We can see if there's a record of how they allocated the areas later. For now . . ."*
You lock on to your own position and see them as the enemy. *"I can't believe this. We've been planning this for months. How could they have messed this up?"*	You move to desired results and work side by side. *"Let's see how we can share the space so we can be ready when our guests arrive. We both want the same thing."*

· Chapter 6 ·

Name the Game

Would you like to know what to do if someone is deliberately trying to manipulate you?

A fundamental law of negotiation states, "A recognized tactic is no longer effective." If you catch someone intentionally trying to undermine you, eliminate their unscrupulous tactics by exposing them.

From this day forward, as soon as you sense someone is playing head games with you, name his game to cancel it. To do this, mentally step out of the situation, ask yourself what is happening, and then state your observation.

MAKE THE COVERT OVERT

"I destroy my enemy by making him my friend."

—ABRAHAM LINCOLN

Tongue Fu! is about finesse, not fighting. Our goal is to neutralize, not destroy aggressors by bringing their negative tactics to light.

My husband was looking for a family car. After visiting car dealerships for several weekends, he found exactly what he wanted. He was ready to sign the contract when the salesman said, "I'll be right back. I've got to clear this price with my manager."

After waiting for almost twenty minutes, my husband realized the employee was pulling the good guy/bad guy routine. The salesman must have noticed how much Les liked the van, so he decided to let him sit for a while. The salesman probably figured that if Les didn't know whether the deal was going to be approved, he'd grow anxious and be willing to pay more.

Sure enough, that was the salesman's intent. He finally returned and insincerely apologized. "Gee, I'm sorry this took so long. I tried to wrangle my boss down, but he insists we get $16,000 for that van. He says we are already giving you a bargain price, and we can't let it go for any less."

My husband named the game. He wanted to make a point, not an enemy, so he calmly and firmly told the salesman, "I know you have the authority to set the price. If you'd like to sell that car, I'm ready to sign a contract for $14,500 right now. If not, I'll have to take my business somewhere else."

The salesman rather sheepishly agreed to the original price, all the while muttering under his breath that he was going to take a lot of guff from his supervisor. He knew he'd been caught out.

THWART TACTICS

"Patience is never more important than when you're on the verge of losing it." —ANONYMOUS

What if people are pressuring you to make a decision? They are probably hoping that in your haste, you'll make concessions you wouldn't otherwise agree to. You can counteract that ploy by saying, "You're not trying to rush me into a decision, are you?" Not anymore, they're not!

A woman approached me before a seminar and said, "I'm taking this course because I'm thinking about quitting my job. I work for a father/son law firm. Mr. Murphy Sr. will give me a stack of invoices to prepare, and fifteen minutes later, Murphy Jr. will stop by my desk and ask me to locate some legal files. An hour later Murphy Sr. gets angry because his invoices didn't get mailed. Meanwhile, Murphy Jr. wants to know where the legal files are. I can't take it anymore. They're driving me crazy."

I recommended she mentally step outside the situation so she could see it objectively. I suggested she ask herself, "What's happening here?" She observed, "They're putting me in the middle."

Then *say* that. The next time one of them gives you a conflicting assignment, speak up! Don't suffer in silence or make best-guess decisions that keep getting you in hot water. Say courteously, "Don't put me in the middle here. Your son [father] has asked me to work on a different project. If the two of you would please agree which has priority, I'll be glad to get started on it."

PERTURBED VS. PATIENT

"Patience is the companion of wisdom."　　　—SAINT AUGUSTINE

In one of my workshops, a bartender said a tough part of his job is getting hit up for complimentary drinks. He said, "I used to lose my patience because freeloaders put me in an awkward position. Now if someone tries to wheedle a freebie out of me, I just say, 'You're not asking me for a free drink, are you?' Or if minors are pressuring me to serve them, I say, 'You wouldn't want me to lose my job by selling drinks to someone under age, would you?' Now that I know what to say, I don't get perturbed anymore when someone puts the squeeze on me for a free beer."

A policeman added, "We use this Name the Game idea a lot. 'You wouldn't be trying to bribe a police officer, would you?' is usually all it takes to stop someone in his tracks if he's on the verge of suggesting something illegal."

Have you ever been the bearer of bad tidings? Did the recipient of the bad news dump his displeasure on you for reporting it, even if you had nothing to do with causing it? Would you like to know how to prevent this?

Adopt the "Why are you taking it out on me?" posture. Shrug your shoulders, put both palms up and out in a "Why me?" gesture, and say plaintively, "Hey, don't shoot the messenger."

"Anger is momentary madness," observed the great poet and satirist Horace. Most people will stop making you the object of their anger if they're made aware of their madness. They'll say something like "I know. It's not fair to blame you. It's just this is the last thing I needed to hear today." Or they'll apologize and say, "I'm sorry for taking this out on you. This news just comes at the worst possible time."

BYPASS BICKERING

"Don't fight forces. Use them."   —R. BUCKMINSTER FULLER

To paraphrase Bucky Fuller, don't fight forces, name them. Have you ever taken a long drive in the car with your family? Do you start out like the Waltons and end up like the Simpsons? If everyone starts bickering, remember to articulate rather than get angry about what's happening. "We're all hot and tired because we've been crammed in this car for four hours. We'll be at the hotel in a few minutes. Let's be civil to each other until then."

A woman offered, "My fiancé and I use a variation of the Name the Game idea. When we first met, he would ask me about the guys I used to go out with. He would become jealous. Then I'd get upset with him for bringing up something I didn't want to talk about in the first place. It was breaking us apart.

"Last month we agreed not to discuss the people we previously dated. We're getting along great now because we don't bring up former girlfriends or boyfriends. If we run into someone we used to see socially, we just look at each other and say, 'History.' That one word keeps us from falling back into our old habits."

You've probably heard the popular saying, "Unless we learn from our history, we're doomed to repeat it." This couple has not only learned from their history, they've learned that *naming* their history prevents them from repeating it.

VOICE THE VISCERAL

"Wit is the only wall between us and the dark."
—MARK VAN DOREN

Perhaps the best demonstration of Name the Game I've ever witnessed was given by popular radio announcer Karl Haas. Haas hosts a program called *Adventures in Good Music,* which is broadcast on many public radio stations. Haas's deep bass voice is in itself a beautiful instrument, rich and resonant in tone, an immediately recognizable vocal signature.

Haas came to Hawaii several years ago to present a concert for his many fans. The auditorium was filled with several hundred of his loyal listeners, all eager to see their radio hero in person. The theater darkened, the stage lit up, everyone applauded enthusiastically, and out walked—to the crowd's astonishment—a very short Karl Haas.

Everyone gasped. The radio personality had obviously received this startled reaction before and was ready with a witty response. A twinkle in his eye, he leaned toward the audience and confided, "I didn't know what *you* looked like, either!"

The audience roared. His clever handling of this potentially uncomfortable situation won over everyone in the room. The beauty of Haas's Fun Fu! remark was that it named the game by expressing what everyone was thinking.

This technique of saying the unsayable works particularly well with children. I'll always remember our boys' first, very reluctant visit to the dentist. The friendly doctor came out to greet them, hunkered down to their level, and said, "I bet you don't want to be here, do you?"

Their eyes widened as he expressed exactly how they were feeling. "In fact, I bet you want to turn around and run right back out that door, don't you?" They nodded in unison as he continued to voice their every fear. A minute later, they each took one of his hands and happily headed into the examination room with this man who so obviously understood how they felt. By articulating their apprehensions, he had neutralized their fears.

ACTION PLAN FOR NAMING THE GAME

You are the first female to work with a formerly all-male crew, and they are testing you. Some of them are telling jokes that are in questionable taste; others are intentionally giving you technically difficult jobs to see if you're up to the task. What do you do?

WORDS TO LOSE	WORDS TO USE
You let their tactics get to you and become irritated. *"This is infantile behavior. Why don't you grow up?"*	You recognize what they're doing and choose to stay calm. *"This just comes with the territory. I can handle it."*
You allow them to intimidate you. *"I don't know how much longer I can stand this. I dread coming to work."*	You resolve that they are not going to make you a victim. *"I have a lot to offer, and I spent a lot of time and money training for this job. I'm not going to let them scare me off."*
You let your voice become emotional, which tells them they've won. *"I can do the work just as well as you can. Why do you have to make things so rough?"*	You can speak in a calm, confident voice, with a trace of knowing humor. *"You wouldn't be testing me now, would you?"*
You weakly defend yourself, which only rewards their bullying. *"Come on, guys. Give me a break. Why don't you just leave me alone and let me do my work?"*	You name the game, letting them know that you are aware of what they're trying to do. *"Checking me out, are you? I figured you'd want to see if the 'little lady' was up to the job."*

> "THE REAL ART OF CONVERSATION IS NOT ONLY TO SAY THE RIGHT THING IN THE RIGHT PLACE, BUT TO LEAVE UNSAID THE WRONG THING AT THE TEMPTING MOMENT."
> —DOROTHY NEVILL

· Chapter 7 ·
Tongue Glue

A popular T-shirt in Vermont has this legend: DON'T TALK UNLESS YOU CAN IMPROVE THE SILENCE. Wise advice, isn't it?

It can be hard to keep quiet when you've been wronged. You may feel like telling the person responsible off. As Henry Ward Beecher said, though, "Speak when you're angry—and you'll make the best speech you'll ever regret." This chapter teaches you how to hold your tongue (Tongue Glue) so it doesn't get you into trouble.

TACT EQUALS TONGUE IN CHECK

"It is better to swallow words than to have to eat them later."
—FRANKLIN D. ROOSEVELT

A seminar participant burst out laughing when I read the Roosevelt quote. He had learned this the hard way on a blind date. "In the first few awkward moments of exchanging life histories, I discovered my date used to live in my hometown. She asked if I had known Mrs. Walford, and without thinking I said, 'That old hag? She was my high school English teacher.'

"I explained that I had hated her class and that she had flunked me. I noticed too late that my date had a funny expression on her face. When I finally wound down, she said, 'Mrs. Walford is my stepmother.' Argghh! The evening went downhill from there and couldn't have been over soon enough for either of us."

If only that young man had read Oscar Wilde before he went on that blind date. Wilde gives this description of one of his characters: "He knew the precise psychological moment when to say nothing." So before you mouth off, ask yourself if what you want to say could come back to haunt you. If there's a possibility it could backfire, keep it to yourself.

SILENCE AS A DIPLOMATIC TOOL

"A diplomat is someone who thinks twice before saying nothing."
—ANONYMOUS

Let's use the example of a job interview to illustrate when and why it's wise to keep your own counsel. Imagine the interviewer asks if you liked your former supervisor. Pretend the friction between you and your previous manager was the reason you resigned from the company.

Bad-mouthing your former boss, no matter how much he deserves it, would only reflect poorly on you. As Will Durant noted, "To speak ill of others is a dishonest way of praising ourselves." Even if the interviewer agrees with your observations, he will think less of you for being indiscreet. He may worry that someday you will make the same kind of disparaging remarks about him. As a saying posted on a church bulletin board put it, "Anyone who gossips *to* you will gossip *about* you."

In this case, silence is indeed the better part of valor. Valor is defined as "strength of mind or spirit that enables a person to encounter danger with firmness." Resolve to act with integrity. Refuse to give in to the urge to (as we say in Hawaii) "talk stink." No one will respect you for trashing a former employer. If you must say something, make it constructive. Sum up the relationship by saying, "I learned a lot from him/her." This statement is undoubtedly true and is a more gracious way to express your feelings.

KEEP QUIET

"Silence is the purveyor of power."　　　　　—TONGUE FU'ISM

Would you like to know another use for silence?

If someone is being stubborn, a pause coupled with the question "So what do you suggest?" is an excellent way to persuade them to see your point of view.

Years ago, I was asked by the University of California at Los Angeles to present a workshop on concentration. I arrived at my hotel the evening before the program and asked for the box of handouts I expected to be waiting for me. The staff, after much searching, reported they couldn't find it. My only option was to re-create and duplicate the material that night.

This was before convenient twenty-four-hour copy centers, so I was stymied until I spied a computer and Xerox machine in the hotel office. I explained my situation and asked to use their equipment. I promised to take good care of their property and offered to pay for its usage.

The front-desk manager turned me down flat. In fact, you can guess his rationale for rejecting my request: "If we let *you* use our computer, we'd have to let *everybody* use our computer."

I understood his reluctance. He didn't know if I would misuse the equipment, and it was easier to say no than to say yes. I knew if I gently persisted this could be a win-win situation, so I used the technique that has the power to move people out of a fixed position. I asked, "So what do you suggest?" and *stopped talking.*

The manager hemmed and hawed while I bit my tongue to keep from rescuing him. My silence compelled him to look at the situation from my point of view. It helped him own the problem so he felt some obligation to resolve it rather than brushing me off with a perfunctory refusal.

Finally he relented. "All right, you can use our computer and Xerox machine. Just be careful!" I did, and I was.

I also took the time to write a letter to the general manager singling out the employee's special service and expressing my appreciation for his assistance in my time of need. That follow-up letter was an important part of the process. I am not suggesting you use silence to unfairly get what you want. I believe such questions as "What do you suggest?" "What would you do if you were in my place?" and "How would you feel?" followed by silence are fair tools *if* you return the favor and keep your side of the bargain. They're *reverse* Empathy Phrases in that they cause the other person to see your perspective. You can use this method to get what you want as long as you're mindful of the other person's contributions and don't take advantage of his largesse.

Silence can be more persuasive than the most eloquent speech. If I had lambasted the hotel manager with all the reasons he should let me use his computer, I would have cemented his resistance. The longer I verbally strong-armed him, the more stubborn he would have become. Persistence can indeed pay off, yet it can also backfire. The squeaky wheel sometimes gets the grease, but sometimes it simply gets replaced.

SILENCE VS. STRONG-ARMING

"There is much to be said for not saying much." —FRANK TYGER

A portrait photographer who had recently moved her headquarters into a new office building called to report her success with this technique. Twice Sue had made an appointment to get new carpet installed, and both times the contractor had called at the last minute to cancel the appointment. They finally agreed to do the work three days before her grand opening. The big day arrived and she waited patiently for the workers. The agreed-upon hour came and went. Another two hours passed before the crew chief called to explain they were running behind (again!) and wouldn't be able to do the job until Monday.

Sue said she was about to let him have it when she remembered a better course of action was to hold him responsible with a question and silence. She said calmly and firmly that another delay was not acceptable, asked, "How would you feel if I had canceled on you three times?" and then clammed up. That question helped him face the fact that her refusal to accept another delay was justified.

The contractor tried once more to repeat his excuses. This time Sue asked, "What do you suggest I do with the seven sittings scheduled for Monday?" She gently persisted with her questions and the subsequent silence, refusing to rescue him. He finally installed the carpeting as agreed that day.

Sue said, "Before Tongue Fu!, I would have been reluctant to press the point. I would have caved in, said it was okay to postpone, and ended up victimized once again. The workshop taught me to be comfortable with a verbal vacuum, instead of rushing to fill it. As a result, I don't let people off the hook and allow them to take advantage of my easygoing nature."

WHEN TO USE SILENCE

"Silence is one of the hardest arguments to refute."   —ANONYMOUS

Being comfortable with a long pause is especially important in negotiations. Imagine, once again, that you're interviewing for a job and you're asked for your salary requirements. If you tentatively reply, "Thirty-five thousand?" the interviewer will know you can be negotiated down. At that point, he may use silence on you and raise his eyebrows in a sign of disbelief as if to say, "You've got to be kidding."

Confronted with this reaction, you may retreat and add weakly, "But I'll take thirty thousand because I really want to work here." Or you may hasten to justify that figure with "That's what I was making before" or "That's commensurate with salaries for similar positions at other companies." Your eagerness will be seen as a clear indication you're willing to take less.

If, instead, you state "Thirty-five thousand" in a sure voice, your speech ending with a downward inflection, your demand will be perceived as firm. If the interviewer tests you by not saying anything, maintain your poise. Sophisticated interviewers know the ability to stay silent under pressure indicates strength of character and a maturity that will make you an asset to their organization.

I believe Tongue Glue is one of the most important Tongue Fu! skills. Confucius wisely observed that "silence is a true friend who never betrays." You can be a friend to yourself by learning how to stay silent in situations where speaking would hurt, not help.

ACTION PLAN FOR TONGUE GLUE

You are part of a community association that is in the process of raising money for a swimming pool. You're attending the monthly meeting, and board members are griping because the committee chair hasn't taken any action. The discussion of the chair's lack of performance turns personal, and several attendees bring up rumors they've heard through the grapevine about a pending bankruptcy and divorce. You're asked your opinion of the man's integrity. What do you do?

WORDS TO LOSE	WORDS TO USE
You speak before considering whether what you're going to say will hurt. *"I think he's dropping the ball on this project. We're way behind."*	You think before you speak so you don't say something you'll regret. *"Will it help if I chip in with my opinion?"*
You join in on the gossip and contribute your negative experiences. *"I heard his wife moved out of their house, and took the three kids and the dog."*	You act with integrity and choose not to bad-mouth. *"I'm going to keep quiet. I don't have any firsthand knowledge as to why he hasn't made progress on this."*
You put in your two cents worth, speaking ill of him in a way that could come back to haunt you. *"He's untrustworthy. What she saw in him, I'll never know."*	You redirect the conversation to a more constructive topic, and refocus the group's attention on other agenda items. *"We have only half an hour left. Let's move on to next point."*

> ## "I HAVE NEVER BEEN HURT BY ANYTHING I DIDN'T SAY."
> —CALVIN COOLIDGE

· Chapter 8 ·

What to Say When You Don't Know What to Say

Would you like to know what to say when someone pulls the verbal rug out from beneath you?

First, it's important to know what *not* to say if you're floored by someone's hurtful remark. Don't try to defend yourself with "That's not true," and don't deny their negative statement with "I don't agree with that!"

Why? If someone hits you with an unexpected verbal blow and you lash back with an indignant denial, you've bought into his broadside. If someone says, "Why are you always on the defensive?" and you reply, "I am *not* on the defensive!," you've just substantiated his statement. If someone accuses a woman of being overly emotional and she objects with "I am *not* emotional!" she has just unintentionally proved the point.

STOP USING STOP

"The mind is literal and is unable to focus on the reverse of an idea."
—TONGUE FU'ISM

A participant in one of my workshops objected, "This doesn't make sense. How can saying something *isn't* true corroborate it?" Great question! Understand that the mind doesn't conjure up the opposite of what's said. It hears what it hears. If you tell it *not* to do something or to *stop* doing something, it will produce the very thing you're trying to avoid. A simple exercise demonstrates this:

> *Please do* not *picture a tall fountain glass filled with a mouth-watering hot fudge sundae. Do* not *picture the mounds of delicious, melted chocolate rolling down the sides of the rich vanilla ice cream. Stop* your mind from think- *ing about the stack of frothy white whipped cream topped with a bright red cherry. Don't* imagine dipping your long spoon into that delectable combination of yummy flavors, bringing it up to your lips, tasting it with the tip of your tongue.

Can you *not* do it? Your mind focuses on the word pictures and doesn't heed the directives *not, stop,* and *don't.* That is why championship athletes visualize what they want ("Get this first serve in") instead of what they don't want ("Don't double fault"). That is why professional coaches say, "Swing slow and steady," instead of "Stop swinging so fast." That is why musicians tell themselves to play softly rather than not so loud.

Use only positive words when talking to others and when talking to yourself. If a coworker warns, "Now don't get mad . . ." and you reply, "I am *not* mad," you'll be imprinting that perception. If someone tells you to stop being a wimp and you answer, "I am not a wimp," your use of his negative word reinforces the unflattering image.

Richard Nixon learned this the hard way. Remember when he gave the Checkers speech following allegations he had taken advantage of his office for personal gain? In a nationally televised interview, he tried to dispute these negative accusations by protesting, "I am not a crook." His attempt to repudiate this characterization did not help his status and only further solidified that unfavorable perception in some people's minds.

This very important concept applies to all communication. A local television anchor closed his show one evening with the homily "There's one sure way to make someone worry. Tell them *not* to." The same is true of other undesirable behaviors. What do you think will happen if you warn rowdy children to "stop fighting"? What will happen if you try to compose yourself by saying, "I am not going to cry"? What will happen if you tell employees to "stop coming in late"?

From this day forward, phrase communication to yourself and others positively: "The two of you need to treat each other with respect." "I will keep a Mona Lisa smile on my face." "Starting Monday, you need to be on time. When I say on time, I don't mean on the property getting a cup of coffee, I mean at your desk ready to take phone calls at eight A.M. sharp."

ANSWER A QUESTION WITH A QUESTION

"The greatest remedy for anger is delay."   —SENECA

So how do you respond if someone takes the words right out of your mind? Put the conversational ball right back in their court with the phrase "What do you mean?" The beauty of that question is that it works on several levels. Asking "What do you mean?":

- Gives you something to say.
- Delays your anger and prevents you from reacting to the attack.
- Reveals the underlying issue so you can address what's really going on.
- Gives you time to compose yourself and collect your thoughts so you don't say something you'll regret.
- Serves as an intelligent rather than an immature response.

It's said envy is almost always based on a complete misunderstanding of the other person's situation. So is anger. A participant in a previous class volunteered, "I used this last week and didn't even realize it. All I know is, it worked!" She went on to explain the situation.

"I was promoted from the ranks six months ago, and I'm now supervising my former peers. It's a delicate situation, to put it mildly. One of my favorite employees walked into my office just before quitting time on Friday, closed the door, sat down, and told me he thought I was doing a terrible job as a supervisor.

"I was flabbergasted. I pride myself on my people skills. I was about to explain I was doing the best I could, but I realized that would just come across as rationalization. Instead, I asked what he meant.

"He said, 'Well, nobody knows what's going on anymore. We haven't had a staff meeting in weeks.' I realized that lack of communication was what he was upset about, so we talked about how to keep everyone informed instead of whether or not I was a good supervisor."

IGNORANT VS. INFORMED?

"Behind every argument lies someone's ignorance."
—LOUIS D. BRANDEIS

A friend called a while back to say thanks. "My six-year-old marched up to me and announced he hated me and wished I wasn't his mother. I was so hurt. My first thought was 'You ungrateful child, how can you say that to me after all I've done for you?' I realized that wouldn't help and remembered your suggestion to answer accusations with a question. So I asked "What do you mean."

"He sobbed, 'All my friends get to stay overnight at the slumber party, and I have to come home. It's not fair.' Having uncovered the real reason he was upset, I was able to clarify that the reason he couldn't sleep over was that we needed to leave early the next morning for his hockey game. Those four words kept me from putting my foot in my mouth and helped us have a decent discussion instead of my blindly reacting to his hurtful comment."

SEEK THE SOURCE VS. REACT TO THE SURFACE

"Ignorance is a voluntary misfortune." —ANONYMOUS

The following anecdote gives further insight into why it's important to uncover what's causing a troublesome situation.

A schoolteacher walked into her classroom after a rainy weekend and discovered a puddle of water in the middle of the floor. She called the janitor and told him what was wrong. He came and mopped up the puddle. The next morning the scenario was repeated.

When the teacher walked in the third day to find yet another puddle, she called the head custodian and explained, "This is the third day in a row this has happened. Could you please come and take care of it?"

When the wizened maintenance supervisor showed up a few minutes later, he didn't even have a mop. The teacher asked with a puzzled look, "How are you going to mop up the puddle?" He replied, "I'm not. I'm going to fix the leak."

Too often when someone says or does something unfair or unkind, people "mop up the puddle." They react to what's happening on the surface instead of seeking the source of the problem and repairing that.

READ THEIR MIND

"Tact is, after all, a kind of mind-reading."

—SARAH ORNE JEWETT

Several years ago, I attended a wedding rehearsal. In the middle of the practice procession down the aisle, the five-year-old flower girl threw a tantrum and refused to continue. The mother took her daughter outside in an effort to discipline her.

They reentered the church a few minutes later only to have the child act up again. The embarrassed mother alternated between pleading for cooperation and issuing dire threats. Neither approach worked and the child continued to pout.

The bride and groom were running out of patience when the girl's grandmother finally inquired, "Lisa, did you have a nap today?" The little girl shook her head. Aaahhh! The real reason for her misbehavior. The older woman knew the obviously tired and overstimulated child needed sleep, not scolding. She gathered her granddaughter into her arms, took her to a pew in the back of the church, and sang her a soothing lullaby. The girl was asleep within minutes.

I felt fortunate to witness the grandmother's wise handling of a tense situation. The mother was reacting to the behavior, frantically mopping up the puddle only to have it reappear. By "mind-reading," being sensitive to what the little girl was feeling, the grandmother was able to figure out what was really going on and deal with it. It was a perfect example of someone who fixed the leak and eliminated the puddle.

What does this mean for you? If someone is misbehaving, you have a choice. You can complain or you can ask questions. You can often clarify the cause of the problem by putting the conversational ball back in their verbal court. "Why do you think that?" and "What do you mean?" are legitimate ways to identify the source of undesirable behavior, which can then be addressed.

ACTION PLAN FOR WHAT TO SAY
WHEN YOU DON'T KNOW WHAT TO SAY

Imagine you've had a hard day at work. All you can think about is coming home, kicking your shoes off, and relaxing in peace and quiet. As soon as you walk in the room, you can tell your spouse is upset. Over dinner you ask what's wrong and she blurts out, "We never do anything fun anymore." This is the last thing you want to hear tonight, and you don't know what to say.

WORDS TO LOSE	WORDS TO USE
You give an emotional denial (which may set up a "Yes, we do/No, we don't" argument). *"We went to the county fair last weekend."*	You find out what's really going on. *"What do you mean?"*
You answer out of ignorance and respond immaturely. *"We go out more than most couples."*	You take the intelligent option and seek information. *"Why do you say that, hon?"*
You try to prove her wrong and engage in verbal warfare. *"Didn't I take you out to dinner and go to that movie you wanted to see?"*	You avoid a word war by not defending yourself. *"What makes you think that?"*
You can react to what's happening on the surface and miss the point. *"Listen, I work fifty hours a week. I don't have the energy to go out and do stuff."*	You can seek the source of the outburst and fix the leak. *"So Barb and Bill are taking line dancing lessons, and . . ."*

· Chapter 9 ·

Find Solutions, Not Fault

Have you ever been part of a group discussion that deteriorated into name-calling and fault-finding? Not pleasant, is it?

A woman said she had been in the middle of a blaming free-for-all the day before. "We were in our monthly staff meeting and our boss asked for the budget reports. Our accountant grimaced and reluctantly confessed he didn't have them. Our CEO demanded to know why.

"The accountant claimed it wasn't his fault; the marketing division hadn't submitted their final figures. The marketing director objected that he wasn't the one who had held things up; he'd been waiting for the forecasts and they'd been sitting in data processing for a week. The DP rep said she had just received the paperwork a couple of days before, and hadn't been able to sign off on the numbers because her supervisor was out of town . . . and back and forth they went."

HALT HOSTILITIES WITH THIS HAND GESTURE

"See problems as holes in the ground. You can dig deeper, or you can break new ground."
—ANONYMOUS

From this day forward, understand that arguments have no constructive value. If you find yourself in a war of words, put your hand up (with fingers pointing skyward, palm facing forward) and stop what's happening with the sentence "Let's not do this."

Why use a hand gesture? It is the most effective way to get attention. If everyone is talking at once, no one can hear the voice of reason. Holding a hand as a police officer would to stop traffic is a universally understood signal to cease and desist. Athletes can probably think of an alternate signal used in the sports world to stop unruly behavior. The T sign coaches and team captains use to call for a time-out is another way to stop the action.

Move the group onto higher ground by focusing on solutions. Say, "We could spend the rest of the afternoon arguing about why this wasn't completed, but that won't help us get the budget reports done on time. Instead, let's focus on how we're going to finish these today."

A city councilman said, "Normally I agree with this, but aren't there times you *have* to assess blame? Our county recently went through an embarrassing financial scandal. If we don't indicate who is responsible for embezzling the funds, we'll all take the fall."

This public official had brought up an important point. In some litigious professions, you need to be cautious about indirectly accepting blame so you don't open yourself to lawsuits (Tongue Sue!). If you're in this situation, be sure to indicate that you are being forced to point the finger and that it is not your normal style. You can say, "I wish I didn't have to do this because I don't like to operate this way. Yet these unfortunate circumstances demand that we name the individual responsible for these illegal deeds so he will be held accountable for his actions. Then I want to focus on how we can keep this from happening again so we can reestablish a reputation of integrity."

PUNISH THE PAST VS. PROFIT FROM IT

"The ultimate in wisdom is to live in the present, plan for the future, and profit from the past."   —ANONYMOUS

Arguments are a waste of time because you can't change the past, you can only learn from it. From this day forward, as soon as people start quarreling, put your hand up and say, "This won't help." Halt the hostilities before they produce casualties. Point out that verbally pummeling each other serves no good purpose; a more productive use of time is to focus on how to accomplish the original objective. Move the group from a "Who did it?" frame of mind to an action-oriented "What can we do about it?" attitude.

A former program attendee reported she'd put this idea into practice with great results. When she and her family walked into their home after returning from spring vacation, they were met by a terrible odor. They finally discovered the source of the smell in the kitchen. Someone had left the refrigerator door wide open and all the food had spoiled.

Her husband demanded, "Who was the last person in the refrigerator?" and the blaming began. "You were the one who fixed a sandwich for the road." "That was before we even left. You were the one who came back in for a soda." "It wasn't me. I wasn't the last one out of the house." Everyone was accusing someone else of being the guilty party.

"Finally," the woman said, "I remembered your technique for putting the past in the past. I raised my hand and shouted, 'Time out!' Then I calmly stated, 'This doesn't help. We could argue until the cows come home about who left the door open, and it won't get this kitchen cleaned up. Instead, let's all pitch in and take care of this mess. When we're finished, we'll figure out a system so when we leave for a trip, someone's in charge of going around to make sure everything is closed up and shut off.' "

ACT AS A VERBAL TRAFFIC COP

"The only way to get the best of an argument is to avoid it."
—DALE CARNEGIE

A participant added this image of how to avoid arguments: "It sounds as if we should act as verbal traffic cops. If people are about to have a communication crash, we're supposed to stop them before they collide in a wreck of rhetoric."

That's true. When a discussion has deteriorated into a heated debate, the participants are headed for hurt. You may be an innocent bystander; however, it's to everyone's benefit for you to prevent the collision.

The key to doing this properly—so that you don't offend anyone—is to use the word *us* or *we*. Your use of the word *you* ("You guys cut this out" or "Why don't you stop passing the buck?") might embarrass the participants in front of their peers and give the impression that you are arrogantly separating yourself from them. By using such collective words as *Let's* or *We'll*, you are acting in the obvious best interests of the group. They will appreciate your intervening on their behalf.

MOVE FROM REASONS TO RESULTS

"At the moment of truth, there are either reasons or results."
—CHUCK YEAGER, AVIATION PIONEER

Glenda, a wise preschool teacher, taught me that my well-intentioned efforts to resolve my sons' squabbles were instead rewarding them. The more often I mediated their disagreements, the more quarrels they had. Why? Their altercations received a lot of attention from Mom. My sons had done a very good job of teaching me how to behave!

Glenda helped me realize that the attempt to find out who is responsible backfires by setting up a victim-and-tattletale syndrome. Digging for details encourages rather than eliminates this unhealthy setup. If kids start fighting, Glenda holds her hand up and asks the students involved to "make silence." "Make silence" is a much more effective command than "Stop talking" because it clearly indicates what the children are to do and imprints the desired behavior. Glenda then separates the children who were fighting, explains their behavior is not appropriate, and asks them to play by themselves until they are ready to treat each other with respect.

Many parents complain in my Tongue Fu! workshops that they have to say things three or four times before their children listen. Parents can reverse the sad state of affairs by *not* repeating themselves. Say, "Children, give me your eyes," which is more compelling and specific than the abstract "pay attention." Pause until everyone is quiet and looking at you, and then state in a firm voice, "I will say this once. Share the toys or they will be put away. Now give each other some space and play like friends."

If a child pipes up with, "But that's not fair. He . . . ," raise your eyebrows, not your voice. Simply put your hand up and open your eyes wide as if to say, "You really don't want to do this, do you?" That is usually enough to let children know you mean what you say. Your refusal to dwell on why a fight started shows children that actions, not excuses, are valued.

SIBLING RIVALRY VS. SIBLING REVELRY

"Do you expect your children to get along, or do you hope they will?"
—JOHN ROSEMOND

One happy mother wrote to say she had used this technique to turn her daughters' sibling rivalry into sibling revelry. She said, "My girls used to snipe at each other constantly. I tried to referee their cat-fights, but instead of making things better, they would get mad at me for taking the other one's side.

"The day after your workshop I called a family conference and explained I would no longer tolerate their senseless squabbles. I used your quote about finding solutions instead of fault, and explained that any time they started in on each other, I was going to stop them. At that point, they would have a choice: they could separate and go somewhere else, or they could focus on what they wanted from each other instead of what they didn't want.

"Of course they tested me. The next day, my youngest daughter threw a fit because her sister had worn her skirt without asking. My older girl accused her sibling of taking her favorite sweater to school, and they were off to the verbal races.

"I put my hand up and said, 'Girls . . .' Do you know I didn't even have to say anything else? Without further prompting, they abandoned their bickering and set up rules about when it was okay to borrow clothes. Holding my hand up was all it took to remind them of our commitment to focus on results, not reasons."

Are you thinking, "I don't have children, so this doesn't apply to me?" A variation of this technique works with people of all ages. Understand that if you try to mediate between two friends who are on the outs, you may end up between the proverbial rock and hard place. Rather than getting drawn into who did what to whom, do everyone a favor and help them shelve the squabble. Put your hand up and say, "Hey, it's over. Let's not spoil our time together by rehashing old news." If you can, get everyone up and out of that room so they can literally and figuratively move on and put it behind them.

ACTION PLAN FOR FINDING SOLUTIONS, NOT FAULT

You are at the store buying groceries. After ringing up your cart-load of purchases, the cashier says your credit card has been re-fused. You didn't bring any checks or cash, so the store manager makes you return the food to the shelves. You are angry at your spouse for not paying the bills as promised and for putting you in this embarrassing position. What do you do?

WORDS TO LOSE	WORDS TO USE
You focus on the past and what went wrong, which serves no good purpose. *"Why didn't you pay the bills like you said you were going to?"*	You focus on the future and how to make it right—which has constructive value. *"Can you pay our Visa account today so I can use our card?"*
You dwell on excuses: why didn't he pay the bills? *"What do you mean, you didn't have time? You should have mailed them last week."*	You turn your attention to what can be done from now on. *"In the future, if we're going to be late paying bills, could you tell me so I don't use our credit card?"*
You bicker back and forth about who is to blame. *"It's your fault I was humiliated in front of everyone at the store. How can you say I should have checked with you first? How was I supposed to know?"*	You halt hostilities by putting a hand up and saying, "Let's not do this." *"Blaming each other won't help. Instead, let's focus on how we can make sure nothing like this happens again."*
You argue about the reasons for the misbehavior. *"It doesn't matter if you've been busy at work. That's no excuse."*	You discuss the results and desired behavior you both want. *"We're on the same side. We both want to keep our account up-to-date."*

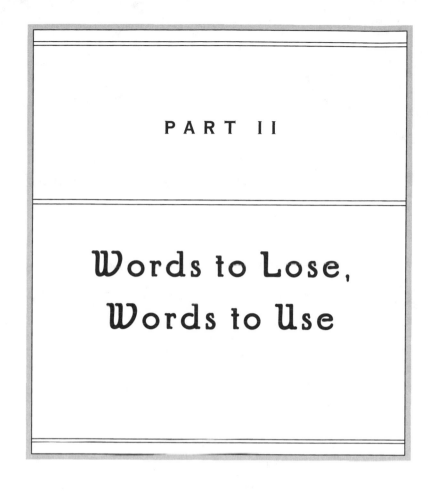

PART II

Words to Lose, Words to Use

> "STICKS AND STONES CAN BREAK MY BONES,
> BUT WORDS CAN BREAK MY HEART."
> —ROBERT FULGHUM

· Chapter 10 ·
Acknowledge, Don't Argue

As Robert Fulghum noted, the children's chant "Sticks and stones can break my bones, but words can never hurt me" is far from correct. Words can wound. In fact, certain words cause people to feel scolded, shamed, judged, or rejected—and they'll respond accordingly.

The chapters in this part of the book identify words that act as weapons. Weapon is defined as "an instrument of offensive or defensive combat: something to fight with." You want to avoid combative words, for they trigger hostile reactions and lead to verbal warfare.

In my workshops, we call this section "Words to Lose and Words to Use." Thousands of people have reported that replacing fighting phrases with friendly phrases has made a dramatic difference in their daily communication—at work, at home, and in the community.

WORDS THAT HELP VS. WORDS THAT HURT

"Words hang like wash on the line, blowing in the winds of the mind."
—RAMESHWAR DAS

While renting a car recently, I watched a situation that dramatically illustrates the damage that can be caused by the first Word to Lose.

A woman approached the rental agent and said, "I'm Evelyn Jones and I've reserved a Ford Mustang." The employee checked his records and said, "Oh yes, Mrs. Jones, we have your reservation right here." Then, his voice faltering, he added, "But we don't have any Ford Mustangs left."

The woman frowned. "How can this be? I phoned several weeks ago to reserve a Mustang." The agent replied, "I see that you did, but we rented them all out this morning."

His customer was not happy. "I don't understand. I took the time to call. You said you'd save one for me."

"I know, but we had a new employee on the desk this morning, and she forgot to read the save list."

When I left, they were still arguing. Why? The car-rental agent kept using the word *but,* a word that negates what's just been said and sets up an adversarial relationship. *But* acts as a verbal hammer and turns discussions into debates.

CONNECTING VS. CANCELING STATEMENTS

"You can't build a relationship with a hammer." —ANONYMOUS

Would you like to know how to construct a wonderful conversation *peace?*

From this day forth, use the constructive word *and* instead of the destructive word *but.* The beauty of this word is that it builds on, rather than blocks out, what has just been said. It advances discussions rather than anchoring them in argument.

The agent could have graciously expedited the transaction if he had said, "You're right, Mrs. Jones, you did reserve a Ford Mustang, and I'm sorry we don't have one available, and I'd like to upgrade you to a higher model. . . ."

Think about it. Doesn't the word *but* often precede negative news? "You did a nice job on this, but . . ." "I know we said it would take only fifteen minutes, but . . ." The word evokes an uh-oh response because listeners know they're about to hear something they'd rather not. "I realize how much you need this loan, but . . ." means "You're not getting the loan." People disregard whatever goes before a *but* because they know that what *follows* the word is what's going to have an impact on them.

The word *and* lets both statements stand, even if they are diametrically opposed to one another. "You did a nice job on this, and could you please add a sentence asking them if they could . . ." "I know I said it would take only fifteen minutes, and I'm sorry it's taking longer. Our computers will be back on line shortly, and then we can . . ." "I would like to grant your loan request, and if you could provide tax records of . . ."

BUT ERASES, AND ACKNOWLEDGES

"Of course I'm yelling. That's because I'm wrong!"
—LESLIE CHARLES

This quote could be modified to read, "Of course I'm yelling. That's because you're making me wrong!" The word *but* minimizes the importance of what someone has just said. "That's a good point, but . . ." is essentially saying "You're in error." The person who has just had his statement discounted is likely to protest.

An English teacher wrote to say what a startling discovery this was for her.

> I've been an educator for twenty years. I've always thought and taught that the word "but" is a conjunction that joins sentences or phrases. You showed me it doesn't join sentences, it jars sentences. I looked up the word "jar" and it means a "state of discord or conflict." "But" doesn't connect statements, it sets up a conflict between them because it doesn't give equal value to what's said before and after it.
>
> My classes studied how this word is used and they all

came to the same conclusion . . . "but" means bad news. "I know you want to use the car, but . . . ," "I'd like to add you to the team, but . . . ," "You almost passed the test, but . . . ," "I want to go to the prom with you, but . . ."

My students and I have resolved to get rid of the "Bad News But." I brought this up to my fellow teachers at our weekly meeting and they've all agreed to change their curriculum to reflect this "revolutionary" insight. It's clear to me that our mandate to teach language goes beyond spelling, pronunciation, and grammar. It also includes selecting words that support rather than sabotage our efforts to communicate constructively.

DIFFERENCES OF OPINION VS. DEBATES

"The test of a first-rate intelligence is the ability to hold two opposed ideas in the mind at the same time." —F. SCOTT FITZGERALD

A variation on Fitzgerald's observation is that the test of a first-rate relationship is the ability of the people involved to hold opposing ideas at the same time *without* becoming opponents. It can be done as long as the couple uses the word *and.* As soon as one person uses the word *but,* the implication is "my way is better than your way, and your way is wrong."

I sometimes ask participants in my workshops to pair off, with one partner taking the position that being single is best and the other maintaining that marriage is the only way to go. I ask them to discuss the ideal status with each trying to convince the other to change his mind. A typical conversation runs like this:

"How can you even think of living with the same person all the time? That's so boring. When you're single you have the freedom to go where you want when you want with whoever you want."

"Yeah, but that gets old after a while. What's really great is to know you've got someone who cares whether or not you come home at night."

"But marriage means you're trapped. If you want to get out, you're locked into mortgages, bills, and alimony."

"Maybe, but your yuppie lifestyle is so frivolous. There's more to life than partying every night."

After five minutes, I stop the exercise and ask participants for feedback. They usually observe that even though they were playing a role, they found themselves getting increasingly exasperated with their partner. I ask how often the word *but* came up. Many of them realize they employed it almost every time they spoke. Without being aware of it, they refuted what the other person said before offering their point of view. They realized that use of the word *but* sets up a Ping-Pong style of conversation in which neither person really listens.

I ask them to continue the discussion, substituting *and* for *but*. Without deliberately trying, they find their conversation becoming more courteous and less contentious.

"You're right, it is fun to be spontaneous and to do things on the spur of the moment, and it's also nice to have children who think you are the greatest thing in the world."

"I can understand the need to settle down and have more permanence in your life, and wouldn't you prefer to be footloose and fancy-free?"

Participants are amazed at the difference. Instead of trying to make the other person "see the error of his ways," they start acknowledging and treating each other's beliefs with respect.

If you're having a disagreement with someone, you're probably both using the word *but*. *But* perpetuates conflicts, *and* prevents them; *but* causes resentment, *and* creates rapport. From now on, use *and* to connect what's being said and you'll be able to discuss controversial ideas without having your conversation turn into a contest.

ACTION PLAN FOR ACKNOWLEDGE, DON'T ARGUE

You want a dog, your partner doesn't. This has become a heated issue for you, and you've decided to make an all-out effort to prove that having a pet would be a good idea. How do you handle the conversation?

WORDS TO LOSE

You use a weapon word that triggers a negative reaction.
"I know you don't like pets, but I do."

You use the word *but*, which sets up an adversarial relationship.
"You say you don't want the hassle, but I'm the one who's going to be responsible for him."

You continue to use the word *but*, which bogs the discussion down because it cancels what your partner is saying.
"I hear what you're saying, but I don't see why you're being so stubborn about this."

You continue to use the word *but*, which erases your partner's point.
"You say vet bills are expensive, but he's not going to get sick, so stop worrying."

WORDS TO USE

You use positive phrasing to keep the conversation constructive.
"I realize you don't want a dog, and it's important to me."

You use the word *and*, which acknowledges your partner's point of view.
"I realize you don't have the time to walk him, and I'll take care of that."

You continue to use the word *and*, which moves the discussion along and connects what's being said.
"I understand how you feel, and I think we can work it so your concerns don't materialize."

You use the word *and*, which acknowledges your partner's point.
"I hear what you're saying, and we'll make sure he gets his shots so he stays healthy."

· Chapter 11 ·

Become a Coach, Not a Critic

What do you do when someone makes a mistake? Do you correct the person by telling her what she should have done?

Here's a story illustrating the damaging impact of the word *should,* and the dramatic difference using an alternative can make.

My friend Charlie is the football coach at a local high school. Several years ago, his team was tied with another for the league championship. Their final game of the season was a cliff-hanger against the very team they were tied with. The score was 14–14 in the fourth quarter; Charlie's team had the ball and was marching downfield. Their quarterback threw a long pass, and their best receiver (Charlie's son, Johnny) was racing down the sidelines in perfect position to catch the throw.

Just before catching the ball, Johnny did something he'd been told a hundred times *never* to do: he glanced back over his shoulder to see how close the defender was. You know what happened. The football missed his outstretched fingers and fell to the ground. The dismayed teenager trudged back to the bench, his head down and shoulders slumped.

Charlie was so caught up in the emotion of the game, he stood over his son and shouted, "You idiot! You should have kept your eyes on the ball. What were you thinking? That was a touchdown pass. You had the game in your hands, and you blew it."

He continued berating the boy until his dejected son could take no more. Johnny stood up to his dad and said defensively, "Get off my case, Dad. I didn't mean to do it. I never want to play for you again."

The humiliated teen caught a ride home with a friend after the game and went directly upstairs to his room without speaking to his father.

STOP "SHOULDING" ON PEOPLE

"Nothing is a waste of time if you use the experience wisely."
—AUGUSTE RODIN

Charlie called me the next morning to talk about what had happened. He said, "I know I just made matters worse. But what can you say when someone pulls such a dumb stunt?"

I asked Charlie, "Do you know anyone who can undo the past? If someone makes a mistake and we tell them what they did wrong, they will resent us even if we're right because they can't do anything about it.

"Strike the word *should* from your vocabulary—it has little or no constructive value. You've heard the expression *lose face?* Do you know what losing face is? It's losing dignity. If we tell someone what they were supposed to have done, they feel helpless because they can't erase their error.

"When someone makes a mistake you can lash out or you can look for the lesson. Since your son can't take back that missed pass, the only thing he can do is learn from it. Instead of obsessing about what happened and retreating or withdrawing, he can turn that embarrassing moment into a useful experience by extracting the value and moving on."

I ran into Charlie weeks later and he reported that not only had he apologized to his son for blowing up at him, he had used that disappointing occurrence to shape his interactions with the rest of the team and with his family. "I realized that we all make mistakes and that your advice is the difference between being a coach and a critic. Now when someone does something wrong, I don't scold them with the word *should*. I immediately suggest how they can do it right *next time* or *from now on*."

LOOK FOR THE LESSON

"When you're sad, learn something."   —MERLIN

Imagine someone says to you, "You should have completed this paperwork first." "You should have E-mailed that agenda to me." "You should have brought your car in earlier."

Do you feel as if you're being reprimanded? This after-the-fact advice causes resentment because the person is verbally beating a dead horse. Even if what is being suggested is true, it's tactless. The word *should* is the verbal equivalent of a parent shaking an index finger at a child for messing up.

Imagine how you would feel if instead of punishing you for the past, that person focused on the future. Imagine how you would respond if the person pointed out how you could keep the error from happening again, instead of penalizing you for erring in the first place. "Next time, if you could please fill out the paperwork first, we can expedite your visit." "In the future, could you please E-mail the agendas to me in advance?" "From now on, if your oil light comes on, you might want to bring your car in so we can check it before your engine is damaged."

SHAMING VS. SHAPING BEHAVIOR

"The secret of education lies in respecting the pupil."
—RALPH WALDO EMERSON

A participant in one workshop commented, "I think this idea of coaching instead of censuring is an important quality of a leader.

My first supervisor had a plaque above his desk that said, ALL EXPERIENCE IS EDUCATION FOR THE SOUL. He taught me to shape behavior rather than shame it. If my employees do something wrong, I ask what they are going to do about it now instead of dwelling on why they didn't do what they were told to do.

"I had an opportunity to practice what I preach last week. A new employee misused one of our software programs and crashed our computer. It dropped our entire inventory. On top of that, she doubled the damage by not saving our files with backup discs. The *shoulds* were on the tip of my tongue: 'You should have told us you didn't know how to access that database,' 'You should have left the computer on when it bombed instead of shutting it down.'

"Fortunately, my manager's wise advice, 'Shape, don't shame,' kept ringing in my head. Instead of ripping into her and making her feel worse, I asked what she had learned. She confessed she didn't understand how to use the computer, apologized for her costly mistake, and offered to do what she could to make amends. I said it wouldn't do any good to 'cry over spilt records,' and that a better use of our time was to focus on how we were going to retrieve our files.

"She came into my office later that day, thanked me for the way I had handled her blunder, and asked if she could attend training classes so she wouldn't jeopardize our system again. She said, 'If I had done something like this at my previous job, my boss would still be yelling at me. That's one of the reasons I left that company; I couldn't take his abusive behavior anymore. Thank you for treating me like a human being.' "

"It is a common mistake to think failure is the enemy of success," noted Thomas J. Watson, Sr. "Failure is a teacher—a harsh one, but the best. Put failure to work for you." The next time you or someone around you makes a mistake, put it to work *for* you rather than letting it work *against* you. Turn traumatic events into teachers and you can emerge a better, rather than a bitter, person.

ACTION PLAN FOR BECOMING A COACH, NOT A CRITIC

Your child brings his report card home. You're shocked to see he has flunked math. You didn't have any idea he was having trouble with the subject, and you're concerned his failing grade will affect his college eligibility. How do you talk to your son about this?

WORDS TO LOSE	WORDS TO USE
You focus on the mistake and scold him for what he did wrong. *"Why didn't you tell me you were having problems with math?"*	You focus on the lesson and ask how he can do it right. *"What are you going to do to bring this grade up?"*
You use the word *should* and try to make him ashamed of his behavior. *"You should have studied harder instead of watching so much TV."*	You use the words *from now on* and shape his behavior. *"From now on, the TV doesn't go on until homework is finished."*
You use the words *supposed to* and punish him for his past actions. *"You're supposed to ask your teacher for help if you don't understand it."*	You use the words *next time* and prepare him for the future. *"Next time you're not sure how to complete your assignment, please ask for help."*
You criticize him, making him feel like a failure. *"I'm very disappointed in you for slacking off on your studies."*	You coach him, helping him extract what value he can from the situation. *"I know you'll be responsible about your math homework."*

· Chapter 12 ·

Turn Orders into Requests

Do you know anyone who likes to be ordered around? Probably not.

Look at the following phrases: "You'll have to call back." "You'll have to give me your account number before I can verify your balance." "You'll have to ask George." Do you feel an internal growl upon hearing commands prefaced by "You'll have to"? Have you ever stopped to figure out why that's so?

HAVE TO VS. WANT TO

"A man convinced against his will is of the same opinion still."
—ANONYMOUS

From the moment you wake up to the moment you go to bed, there are only two reasons why you do anything. Think about it. People do things only because they *have* to or because they *want* to.

If you *have* to do something (or else you'll suffer the consequences), you will do it. However, you'll act with what I call the

Three Rs: reluctance, resentment, and resistance. (A workshop participant once piped up and said, "If I'm forced to do something, I'll do it . . . with *rage!*" Another participant got in the spirit of things and chimed in, "I'll do it with *revenge!*") Only when you *want* to do something will you take action voluntarily.

That's why it's so important to reframe orders into requests or recommendations. Turning a command into a suggestion moves people from a grudging have-to frame of mind to a more gracious want-to frame of mind.

Imagine how much better you would feel if someone reworded their commands into questions. "She's not in right now. Would you like to call back, or would you prefer to leave a message?" "If I could please have your account number available, I'll be glad to look up your balance." "George is in charge of this project. If you'd like to call him at this number, he can fill you in on what's happening."

Autonomy is defined as "self-directing freedom," or "the quality or state of being self-governing." Everyone wants to be autonomous, and no one appreciates having it taken away. In the examples above, notice how the questions give you the right to make up your own mind and choose your own course of action. You will be more likely to cooperate because you feel you're in charge.

CONTROL VS. CHOICE

"Common courtesy . . . isn't."   —TONGUE FU'ISM

A workshop attendee spoke up and asked, "What if they don't have a choice? I'm not going to ask my employees if they could please attend the orientation. It's not an option, it's an order." Another participant added his opinion: "If I gave my son a choice about cleaning his room, it would never happen."

As with other techniques in this book, this idea is a servant, not a master. Certainly there are times when you must take control and tell people what to do; however, it is in everyone's best interest to communicate those requirements in a way that minimizes conflict. If you articulate commands in a polite way, people will often choose to comply with them.

To comply is "to conform or adapt one's actions to another's wishes to a rule, or to necessity." If you take the time to phrase an order thoughtfully, other people will be more likely to accept your authority. They'll be motivated to cooperate because the rule is being presented as a request, rather than being rammed down their throat.

COMMAND VS. COURTEOUS

"Life is not so short but that there is always time for courtesy."
—RALPH WALDO EMERSON

Look at these before and after examples. See how rephrasing a distasteful demand can make it easier to digest?

ORDER	REQUEST RECOMMENDATION
"You have to come to the employee orientation on Friday. It's required for all new-hires."	"Could you please plan on attending Friday's employee orientation? All our new staff members will be there."
"You have to work with Vern on this project."	"Could you please coordinate with Vern on this report?"
"You have to take out the trash before you can play with your buddies."	"If you'll carry out the garbage, you can play with your friends."
"You have to go to the permit office to pick up that form, and then you have to bring it back for our signature."	"The permit office is on the third floor. If you could get the form there and then bring it back, we'll be glad to approve it."

A secretary wrote to say her manager had attended my workshop and had taken this idea to heart. She had worked for this aggressive individual for years and said his gruff style and habit of barking orders had worn thin. He presented her with a long to-do list every morning, and throughout the day would call out instructions: "Get Manuel's phone number for me." "Angie, I need that agenda in ten minutes." "Bring me those blueprints."

She said, "The day after your program, he wrote on the top of my to-do list, "Angie, could you please . . .' and then bulleted the tasks that needed to be done. Instead of yelling at me from his office, he'd buzz the intercom and ask, 'Do you have Manuel's phone number?,' 'Could you please prepare the agenda for this afternoon's meeting?' or 'Can you bring in the blueprints, please?' A couple of times he actually got up and came to my desk to make his request.

"I was flabbergasted by this turnaround. I finally asked what was going on, and he explained about Words to Lose/Use. Your course motivated him to evaluate how he was communicating with his staff and his family. He realized that over the years he had become so accustomed to being the boss that he had fallen into the habit of bossing around everyone within earshot. He was man enough to realize his dictatorial style had alienated the people who worked for him and lived with him. To his credit, he decided it wasn't too late to teach an old dog new tricks, and he's making a conscious effort to be more courteous when communicating with others. Believe me, it's made working for him a lot more enjoyable."

ADMONISH VS. ASK

"The true aim of everyone who aspires to be a teacher should be not to impart his own opinions, but to kindle minds."
—FREDERICK ROBERTSON

Admonishing is really just another word for nagging. Parents and partners sometimes fall into the trap of following their kids or spouse around, "reminding" them of what needs to be done when.

"You have to find something for show-and-tell tomorrow." "You need to practice the piano so you're ready for that recital." "You'd better get gas tonight, the gauge is on empty." "You have to take care of the plants soon, they're wilting." Although these reminders are meant to be helpful, they come across as reproofs. Recipients of this unsolicited advice will bristle and mentally drag their feet in complying.

A more sophisticated approach is to facilitate self-discovery by asking leading questions that help them arrive at the action to be taken. This requires forethought; but, it is the difference between being an educator and an autocrat. The Latin root of the word *educate* means to draw out. "What are you going to take for show-and-tell?" "How's your music coming along for the recital?" "Is there enough gas to get you to work in the morning?" "Do you think the plants need watering?"

See how these queries elicit action in a "kinder, gentler" fashion? From now on, direct with dignity. Instead of arrogantly doing others' thinking for them, which at some level they will resent, aid them in developing and drawing their own conclusions. Kindle their mind with questions rather than killing their initiative with commands.

ACTION PLAN FOR TURNING ORDERS INTO REQUESTS

You have been appointed volunteer coordinator for a soup kitchen sponsored by a group you belong to. You must make sure everyone knows what to do and how to do it. How do you handle this role?

WORDS TO LOSE	WORDS TO USE
You assume being in charge means giving orders and dictating what's to be done. *"Listen up. Here's a list of what you need to accomplish in the next two hours. You're going to have to hustle to finish on time."*	You understand that leading means courteously motivating people so they choose to comply. *"Thank you for coming today. Let's outline what needs to be done so we're ready by six P.M."*
You start telling people what they are supposed to do, and they start to feel resistant. *"Kathy, you peel the carrots. George, you start the soup, and Alejandra, set out the dishes."*	You rephrase orders as requests so people feel respected. *"Kathy, could you start peeling carrots? George, if you could get the soup going, and . . ."*
You couch your commands as *have-tos*, and people feel bossed around. *"Anthony, you have to have the ovens ready at five-thirty to warm up the main dishes, so make the rolls now."*	You recommend actions, so people feel autonomous and cooperate because they want to. *"Anthony, can you get the rolls finished first so the ovens will be ready for the casseroles?"*

· Chapter 13 ·

Clear Away the "Can't Because" Barrier

How do you feel if someone rejects your request? Imagine asking, "Can I pick up my paycheck early? I'm going to Las Vegas this weekend," and having your supervisor brusquely reply, "No, you can't, because it hasn't been approved by Payroll yet."

Do you see how the words *no* and *can't because* are like verbal doors slamming in your face? Those words create an adversarial relationship between you and the other person because he is not giving you what you want.

How much better you'd feel if instead of telling you what you *couldn't* do, the supervisor focused on what you *could* do and responded, "Yes, you can have your paycheck as soon as it's approved by Payroll." The words *yes* and *as soon as* open the door instead of closing it in your face.

From now on, if someone asks you for something, remember that you can often grant the wish contingent on some small condition. Instead of concentrating on what can't be done and why, figure out how it can be done and when.

Instead of saying, "No, we can't start the game because we're still waiting for the umpire to show up," say, "We can begin the game as soon as the umpire arrives. And if he's not here in five minutes, we'll play ball anyway." Rather than telling someone, "I can't find out if that item is in inventory because our computer is down," tell them, "I can check to see if we have that item in stock as soon as our computer is repaired. They're working on it right now, and with any luck it'll be back on line in a few minutes."

DEPRIVE VS. DEVISE

"It is one of the most beautiful compensations of this life that no man can sincerely try to help another without helping himself."
—RALPH WALDO EMERSON

Deprive means "to take something away from . . . to withhold." If you tell someone she can't do something, you are withholding what she wants and she'll resent you for it. Devise is defined as "to plan to obtain or bring about." Instead of explaining what can't be done, demonstrate how it can be done. Instead of alienating them, assist them. Your sincere efforts to help will benefit you as well.

A single father with three children reported what a difference this had made in his family. He said, "I used to constantly be at odds with my kids. They'd come to me for permission, and I'd say no. I felt like a bad guy turning down every request. 'No, you can't take the car, because I need it.' 'No, you can't have your friends over, because you haven't finished your chores.' 'No, you can't play video games because you haven't done your homework. 'No, you can't have ice cream, you haven't had dinner yet.'

"Your seminar showed me that I don't have to be a big meanie. I can use the phrases *as soon as* or *right after* to let them have what they want, as long as they keep their side of the bargain. 'Sure, you can take the car as soon as I get back from shopping.' 'Yes, you can have your friends over right after you finish your chores.' 'You're welcome to play video games as soon as you get your homework finished.' 'Sure, you can have some ice cream right after we have a healthy dinner.' "

MOVE FROM APATHY TO EMPATHY

"Kind words can be short and easy to speak, but their echoes are truly endless."
—MOTHER TERESA

What if there *is* no "Sure, as soon as . . ." or "Yes, right after . . ."? What if there's no way you can grant their wish? What if there's nothing you can do to help them? Understand that if you persist in using the phrases "there's no way" or "there's nothing," you'll both end up frustrated. You'll feel powerless to accommodate them, and they'll feel you're indifferent to their dilemma.

From now on, soften the blow of bad news with the phrases "I wish" or "I hope." The phrases "there's nothing" or "there's no way" are apathetic. The phrases "I wish" or "I hope" are empathetic. You can't always give people what they want. You can give them your concern so they know you care. Your choice to use kind rather than curt phrasing can, to paraphrase Mother Teresa, echoes endlessly.

Instead of "I can't get your copy in this month's newsletter, it's too late," say, "I wish I could get your copy in the newsletter and it's already at the printers. If you'd like, I can keep it on file and make sure it gets prominent placement next month." Instead of "There's no way we can deliver your supplies this morning. The shipment hasn't arrived yet," say, "I wish we could deliver your order this morning, and our trucks are held up at the docks. I'd be glad to call you the minute it arrives."

Imagine you're trying to get home for the Christmas holidays and the airport is closed due to a blizzard. Suppose the airline employee says, "Look, they've canceled all flights. There's nothing I can about it. You won't be able to get out for the remainder of the morning," or "There's no way a plane can take off in this weather. You'll just have to wait until it clears up." These words would make you feel more, not less, exasperated. The employee appears nonchalant about your predicament.

Now suppose that employee says, "I wish we could get you out on a flight. I know you want to get home for Christmas. What I can do is make an announcement as soon as they reopen the airport," or "I'm sorry the snow is keeping your plane from taking off. There's something I can do: give you a meal coupon so you can buy dinner on us while you're waiting." The phrases "I wish" and "There's something" are doorways. The phrases "I won't be able to" and "There's nothing" are dead ends.

THERE'S NOTHING VS. THERE'S SOMETHING

"It is better to light one candle than curse the darkness."
—MOTTO OF THE CHRISTOPHER SOCIETY

One mother said she couldn't wait to get home to use this "I wish" idea. "My daughter came running into the house last night, twirled me around, and announced she had won the lead in her school play. She told me when opening night was going to be, and asked me to please save the date. I checked my calendar and found I was going to be out of town at a conference that weekend and wouldn't be able to attend. When I broke the news to my daughter, she begged me to change my business plans. I regretfully explained there was no way I could cancel my trip.

"I've missed a lot of my daughter's events because of my traveling, and this was the final straw for her. She accused me of caring more about my work than I did about her. I tried to reassure her that wasn't true, but she wouldn't listen to me.

"I see now that because I insisted there was nothing I could do about it, she felt I was being rigid and insensitive as to how important this was to her. If instead I had said, 'I wish I could be sitting front row center to see you in your shining moment,' she would have understood I wasn't casually bowing out.

"I've realized there's something I *can* do. When I talk to her tonight, I'm going to ask if we can get a friend to videotape the play so we can have our own private showing at home when I get back. We can sit on the couch together, and she can talk me through her performance. That way she'll know I really *do* want to share in and celebrate her accomplishment."

BE SENSITIVE, NOT SARCASTIC

"To commiserate is sometimes more than to give, for money is external to a man's self, but he who bestows compassion communicates his own soul."

—W. H. MOUNTFORD

A park ranger said, "This idea is really going to come in handy for my staff. We're the only point of contact for visitors, so we field all the complaints. We hear about crowded campgrounds, dirty rest rooms, vandalized trail signs. We even get complaints about the mosquitoes!

"I don't know why people take their frustration out on us. We didn't invent mosquitoes; we can't stop crime. What do they expect us to do?

"I can see that instead of shrugging our shoulders and saying, 'There's nothing we can do about the mosquitoes. It's summertime, you've got to expect them,' it would be more sensitive to say, 'You might want to pick up some bug repellent at the park lodge; it helps to keep them away.' Instead of a sarcastic 'There's nothing we can do if headquarters tries to cram three hundred people in on a holiday weekend,' it's more supportive to say, 'I wish there were fewer people, too. If there's any way you can come back in the off-season, it's not so busy then and you can have the trails to yourself.' Instead of cutting them off with a curt 'We can't monitor the bathrooms every minute of the day,' we could commiserate with, 'I'm sorry the rest room was in such deplorable condition.' "

To elaborate on the motto from the Christopher Society, telling people what you can't do or what they can't have is a way of cursing the darkness. Choosing to focus on what you can do and what they can have is a way of lighting a candle with compassion.

ACTION PLAN FOR CLEARING AWAY THE
"CAN'T BECAUSE" BARRIER

You are a travel agent in a busy office and your desk is stacked with UPOs (Unidentified Piled Objects). A client calls with a complicated trip itinerary; she asks you to research the best fares and call her back with the flight schedule as soon as possible. You already have a backlog of work to do and know you won't be able to get her information today. How do you deliver this news?

WORDS TO LOSE	WORDS TO USE
You tell your client what you *can't* do, and she resents having her request rejected. *"I can't research that for you now, I'm overloaded as it is. It will have to wait until tomorrow."*	You tell your client what you *can* do, and she feels her request is being honored. *"I will be glad to look those fares up for you first thing in the morning."*
You deprive her of what she wants and she feels alienated. *"There's no way I can get that information for you now. I have several other clients waiting for tickets."*	You let her know how you're going to assist her, and she feels acknowledged. *"As soon as I process these tickets, your trip will be my first priority."*
You explain why you won't be able to help her. She feels you're apathetic. *"I can't drop everything else and process yours first. That wouldn't be fair."*	You tell her what you wish you could do, and she feels you're empathetic. *"I wish I could handle your request right now, and I need to take care of these."*

· Chapter 14 ·

Become Problem Free

Would you like to know another word that causes problems?

That's it—the word *problem*. For scientists and mathematicians, the word simply means "a question raised for inquiry, consideration, or solution," and it doesn't necessarily have a negative connotation.

For most people, though, the word *problem* means trouble. Webster's defines *problem* as "a source of perplexity, distress, or vexation." If you use this word in everyday conversations, the other person will feel something is wrong, even if it's not. The listener will be perplexed, distressed, or vexed, and you'll have a difficult person on your hands!

PROBLEM EQUALS SOMETHING'S WRONG

"If the only tool you have is a hammer, you tend to see every problem as a nail."
—ABRAHAM MASLOW

A boutique owner broke out laughing when I introduced this Word to Lose. She said, "Last month I went to an entrepreneurial training program and we talked about MBWA (Management By Walking Around). The instructor told us that if we were holed up behind our desks all day pushing paperwork, we were not fulfilling our function as supervisors because we were losing touch with our frontline people.

"That made sense to me because I often get buried under a stack of paperwork, so I vowed to get out of my office every few hours to visit the sales floor and check in with my employees. Guess how I greeted them? 'Any problems?' No wonder it seemed like all I ever heard were gripes. From now on, I'm going to ask, 'How's it going?' or 'What's it been like today?' to open up communication and encourage them to tell me about everything that's happening instead of just the foul-ups."

OPEN VS. OPPRESSIVE COMMUNICATION

"A powerful agent is the right word. Whenever we come upon one of those intensely right words the resulting effect is physical as well as spiritual."
—MARK TWAIN

A man in a Tongue Fu! workshop for parents shook his head ruefully and added, "I wish I had known this last night. My grown son and I don't talk much anymore. He called me and asked, 'Can I talk with you, Dad?' Guess how I responded? 'Sure, son, what's the problem?' I can see now that response must have made him think the only reason he might want to call his old man was because something was wrong."

As Twain observed, words have physical and spiritual consequences. Overuse of the word *problem* can be dispiriting and can actually cause people to avoid you. The best course of action is to use this word only sparingly and judiciously.

CHANGE YOUR WORDS, CHANGE YOUR OUTLOOK

"Our life is what our thoughts make it."   —MARCUS AURELIUS

Our outlook is also what our words make it. A retail professional said, "Our department store has used a modification of this idea with great results. We relabeled our Complaint Department; it is now called Quality Assurance. Changing the name has improved the morale and performance of the people who work there. They used to find their work depressing because all they ever did was field and fix problems. Now they see their job as maintaining excellence. Every comment they receive is an opportunity to improve the quality of our service and products. They take pride in what they do now because they see their efforts as being a positive contribution to our company's reputation."

By substituting positive phrases for the word *problem,* you can change any conversation for the better. Here are some examples:

BEFORE	AFTER
"Shirley, my secretary said you called. What's the problem?"	"Hi, Shirley, what did you want to talk about?"
"It's time to get back to work. Any other problems we need to discuss before we call it quits?"	"Anything else we need to take care of before we wrap up the meeting?"
"I don't have a problem with you taking Friday afternoon off."	"Sure, you can have Friday afternoon off. You deserve it."
"I have a problem with the way you handled that client."	"What happened with Mr. Mappano?"
"No problem. I was just doing my job."	"You're welcome. I was glad to help," or "My pleasure."
"You want to know what your problem is? You never think of anyone but yourself."	"Could you be more considerate of the people around you?"

Kathryn, a woman who with her husband owns a small flower shop, told me that this idea had a long-lasting impact on her husband: "I don't think he realized how much his use of the word *problem* was coloring his perception of life. *Everything* was a problem with Harry.

"If I came back from deliveries and asked how it was going, he'd say, 'It was one problem after another.' Or he'd protest, 'Why does everyone always dump their problems in my lap?' If one of our employees walked into the back room and asked to talk with him, he'd say, 'Sure, what's the problem?' He always wrapped up conversations by saying, 'Any other problems we need to talk about?' If a customer asked if a bouquet could be sent that same day, he said either 'I don't have a problem with that' or 'I have a problem with that.' Yesterday our daughter thanked him for letting her take off early, and he passed off her appreciation with a perfunctory 'No problem.' "

Kathryn had noticed that her husband was innocently and habitually using the word *problem* without comprehending its cumulative, harmful impact.

Kathryn continued: "I bought your audiotape, and we listened to it during our commute. Harry sat absolutely still during the section where you talked about the word *problem*. Then he turned to me and said, 'I do that, don't I?' He vowed to become 'problem free,' and the change has been powerful. You've heard the phrase 'Just because you have a persecution complex doesn't mean everybody's *not* out to get you?' That was him. His frequent use of that 'problematic' word was making him feel life was a burden, a perpetual struggle to prevail against all these hassles out to get him. Eliminating that pessimistic word has given him a more positive outlook. Our family and our customers have really noticed the difference."

NOBODY KNOWS THE TROUBLES I'VE SEEN

"Our attitude is the crayon that colors our world." —ALLEN KLEIN

I agree with Klein's observation, and I also think our words are the crayons that color our attitudes.

ACTION PLAN FOR BECOMING PROBLEM FREE

You have always wanted to be your own boss, so you've started your own computer repair business, which you operate out of your home. Sometimes you can make diagnoses over the phone; other times you need to make house calls. The phone rings and a customer needs helps. How do you respond?

WORDS TO LOSE	WORDS TO USE
You answer the customer's query with the word that carries negative connotations. *"What's the problem with your computer?"*	You respond in a positive, open fashion. *"Hello, Paul, how can I help you?"*
You continue to use the word *problem* and add to his distress. *"It sounds like it's the same problem you had last month. I wonder why it broke?"*	You help him focus on solutions. *"I think I know what's happening. I have time this afternoon if you'd like me to come and look at it."*
You keep bringing up what's wrong, making everything worse. *"Anything else not working with your computer? How about that problem you had with your label printer?"*	You diplomatically seek information without categorizing it as bad. *"Otherwise, how is your computer working? Is the smart label printer cooperating?"*

· Chapter 15 ·
Avoid Going to Extremes

How do you feel when someone uses extreme words? "You *never* listen to me!" "You're *always* late." "*Everything* has to be your way."

Extreme words trigger extreme reactions. As Gibran observed, strong words such as *everyone, all, always,* and *nobody* are often based on truth. When the truth is exaggerated, others often lose their temper. They will vigorously protest all-or-nothing characterizations as being unfair and will be quick to point out the exception.

SPECIFIC VS. SUBJECTIVE

"Precision of communication is important, more important than ever, in our era of hair-trigger balances, when a false or misunderstood word may create as much disaster as a sudden thoughtless act."

—JAMES THURBER

Ground your observations on specific real-life actions to keep your discussion objective rather than subjective. An imprecise put-down such as "You *always* forget to feed the cat. Do you want it to starve?" will produce a passionate denial. This statement is doubly inflammatory because the extreme word is linked to an equally extreme conclusion. It's one thing to complain that your child didn't feed the cat; it's another thing to imply he doesn't *care* about the cat. He's bound to offer a fiery refutation.

Instead, say, "This is the third time this week the cat hasn't been fed. What's happening?" This neutral observation combined with a request for information will focus the conversation on the *incident* rather than the *individual*. Instead of putting your child in a fighting mood, you are giving him an opportunity to explain and correct his actions.

After we had reached just this point in one of my workshops, I caught a woman blushing and asked her what she was thinking. She said, "I've just realized why my kids are tuning me out. In a way, I've destroyed my credibility by exaggerating things. I've fallen into a habit of overstating things: 'Jeffrey, I've told you a million times to close the screen door when you come in from the patio,' or 'Lisa, for the thousandth time, put the milk back in the refrigerator.' "

She then asked, "How do I break the habit?" I recommended she rephrase her complaints into questions that cause her kids to supply the answers. Asking, "Jeffrey, what do you do when you come in from the patio?" and "Lisa, what are you supposed to do with the milk when you're finished with it?" will get better results than harping on what the kids should have done.

Another participant, Rita, a student, said she wished she had her college roommate with her at the workshop. "She thinks I'm a slob. Last night, she accused me of *never* cleaning our place and said that she's *always* picking up after me, that she's tired of being the *only one* who takes care of the apartment."

I asked if what her roommate was saying was true. "Of course not. She conveniently forgets that I do the vacuuming and that I'm the one who cooks dinner and does the dishes every night."

Rita had just pointed out a third reason why all-or-nothing words inflame emotions: they often target prior actions or inactions. This produces a triple whammy—an extreme accusation followed by an unfair conclusion and recrimination for the past.

I suggested Rita direct the extreme words back at her accuser as questions. Feeding the offending words back in a inoffensive way gives her housemate a chance to qualify or quantify her charges and an argument can be prevented. Rita could gently yet incredulously repeat her roommate's sweeping statement—"I *never*... clean the house?"—while raising her eyebrows as if to say, "You can't really mean that." Her roomie would probably back off her inaccurate indictments, grumbling, "Well, last night I spent over an hour putting things away." *Aaahh.* This more factual account of what had caused her roommate's furor might motivate Rita to respond objectively rather than emotionally. She might choose to apologize for leaving a mess and to thank her roommate for straightening up.

BYPASS VS. BELABOR ALLEGATIONS

"The art of being wise is the art of knowing what to overlook."
—WILLIAM JAMES

If Rita anticipated that her roommate would play tough and retort, "No, never! I can't *remember* the last time you cleaned the apartment, and furthermore...," she could choose to sidestep the allegation rather than substantiate it. Belabor means "to explain or insist on excessively," and bypass is defined as "to neglect or ignore, usually intentionally." Rita might find it wiser not to belabor her roommate's remark ("Who do you think you are to call me a slob?"), but to bypass it.

Sandor Minab noted, "Nothing determines who we will become so much as those things we choose to ignore." Rita could choose to overlook the pejorative word *slob* and move the conversation to specific solutions. She could say, "If you want to discuss how we can keep our apartment neater, I'd be glad to talk with you."

DRASTIC WORDS CAUSE CATASTROPHES

"I've suffered a great many catastrophes in my life. Most of them never happened."
—MARK TWAIN

Bill an acquaintance of mine was able to use this idea to change his fiancée's habit of speaking in extremes. "I think words like *worst, terrible,* and *impossible* are extreme words too. Winona is an intense woman, and it shows in her language. She used to say things like, 'That was the *worst* meal I've ever had,' 'I look *terrible* in this dress,' or 'You're *impossible* to talk to.' 'We *never* go any-where anymore.' She would work herself into a funk by using such rile-up words."

He was right. Stress researcher Hans Selye found that "Events don't cause stress; your interpretation of events causes stress." The diagram below can help you visualize how this works.

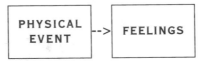

Physical events (i.e., you stub your toe, you jump into an icy cold stream) produce feelings directly. You don't have to think about or decipher what happened. Your toe hurts. Your body gets goose bumps (or as we call them in Hawaii, "chicken skin").

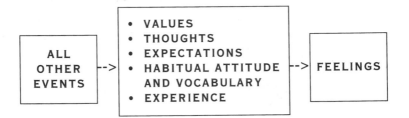

Everything else that takes place (i.e., your TV doesn't work) is processed through your mind, which then produces feelings based on your values, thoughts, expectations, previous experience, and habitual attitude and vocabulary. You may feel anger ("Not now! My favorite program is about to start"), grudging relief ("I'll take this as a sign I should go to aerobics class"), resentment ("Those darn kids have been messing with the remote again"), or general dismay ("Doesn't anything ever work around here?").

MAKE YOUR FEELINGS FIT THE FACTS

"There is nothing either good or bad, but thinking makes it so."
—WILLIAM SHAKESPEARE

As Shakespeare observed, circumstances themselves are not good or bad, it depends on how you interpret them. That is why you must describe precisely what happens so your feelings are appropriate to the situation. If you exaggerate your descriptions, you'll exaggerate your feelings, and perhaps exaggerate the consequences. If your portrayals are excessively negative, so your outlook will be.

How can you make sure your feelings are appropriate to the facts? When something happens, immediately check your thoughts for accuracy by asking yourself, "Is this true?" If you look at a stack of bills and think, "It'll take me a hundred years to pay off all those charges," ask yourself if that's true. If it's not true (and extreme statements rarely are), ask yourself, "What is true?" Be precise. You may realize that what's true is that it will take you three months to retire those debts. You have now correctly assessed the situation rather than catastrophized it.

Bill said that the day after we talked about this idea, he picked Winona up for a date. No sooner had she gotten in the car than she started in with a familiar complaint: *"Nothing* ever goes right . . ." He turned to her and asked, "Winona, is that true? Does *nothing* ever go right?" That question stopped her tirade instantly.

First, she sat in silence for a while. Then she shook her head. "That's not true. There are plenty of things that go right."

"We continued to talk about this habit of 'awfulizing' and how drastic words make things worse than they are. We agreed to keep each other honest in the way we react to situations. If we slip up and represent something as being terrible, we ask ourselves, 'Is that true? What is true?' If we see a movie we don't like, that doesn't mean it was horrible. If I forget to order mushrooms on our pizza, that's not a capital crime. If she breaks a nail, it's not a disaster. We substitute more neutral words like *interesting* and *inconvenient* for negative words like *dreadful* and *unforgivable*.

"We've even stopped using the words *hate* and *kill*. It's become almost a fad to say 'I hate it when that happens' or 'I'm going to kill him for that' when anything goes wrong. Those are such violent words, we've decided we don't want these vicious images creeping into our vocabulary. We see events more clearly now rather than categorizing everything as a calamity. It's made our relationship and our time together more enjoyable."

What negative, violent words have crept into your vocabulary? The insidious ("having a gradual and cumulative effect") impact of these negative images is that they turn one into a pessimist, described by Galsworthy as "one who is always building dungeons in the air." Commit to using more positive images and you can climb out of those self-made dungeons and see the world as the wonder it is.

ACTION PLAN FOR AVOIDING GOING TO EXTREMES

You and your teenagers go to the video store to rent a couple of movies for the weekend. Your children select an R-rated film, and you tell them they need to pick something less violent. How do you respond to their statement that you *never* let them watch what they want?

WORDS TO LOSE	WORDS TO USE
You deny their accusation and establish yourself as an adversary. *"That's not true, and you know it. Last week you picked both movies."*	You repeat their extreme statement with an upward inflection. *"I never let you pick the movie you want to see?"*
Your kids say, "You always make us get a Disney movie," and you refute what they've said. *"That's ridiculous. We haven't seen a Disney movie in months."*	You direct their all-or-nothing accusation back at them as a question, then say nothing else. *"I always make you get Disney movies?"*
They add an extreme conclusion and say you never care what they want anyway, and you feel even more falsely accused and react angrily. *"I do too care what you want. Why do you think we came to this video store in the first place? Not because I want to watch a video."*	You bypass their allegation instead of belaboring it and choose to focus on solutions. *"I know you can find something you'll enjoy watching. What's a movie you'd like to see that's rated PG-13?"*

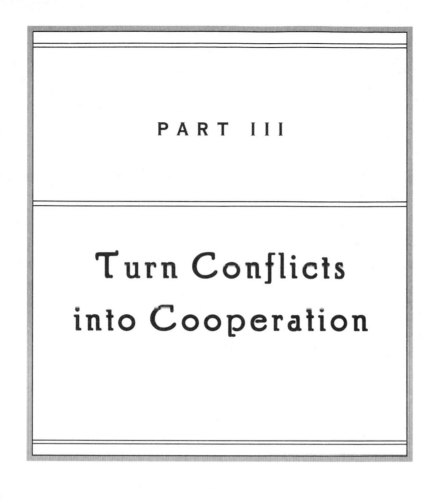

PART III

Turn Conflicts
into Cooperation

> "ONE FRIEND, ONE PERSON WHO IS TRULY
> UNDERSTANDING, WHO TAKES THE TROUBLE TO
> LISTEN TO US AS WE CONSIDER OUR PROBLEMS, CAN
> CHANGE OUR WHOLE OUTLOOK ON THE WORLD."
> —ELTON MAYO

· Chapter 16 ·

Listen Up!

Can you name someone who *really* listens to you? What makes that person such a good listener? How do they make you feel when they gift you with their *undivided* attention? How do you feel about them?

I'm going to guess that out of the hundreds of people you know, you may be able to think of only one or two who really listen to you. It's that rare. Do you realize that concentrating completely on someone is the single best thing you can do to make that person feel significant? Giving your full focus to an individual is a way of saying, "You're the most important thing in my world right now."

Yet most people are so busy that they rarely give their total attention to anyone. In fact, it's said the only people who listen to both sides of an argument are the neighbors! Misunderstandings, mistakes, hurt feelings, conflicts, and disagreements result from this failure to listen.

PARTIAL VS. PATIENT ATTENTION

"Most anger is a cry for attention."   —TONGUE FU'ISM

In the next five chapters, I'm going to outline specific steps you can take to *really listen* to people. By following these suggestions, you can often prevent people from becoming argumentative because they'll have what they want—your ears. These techniques can also help you soothe someone who's already upset.

How? People become difficult in order to capture your attention. If someone realizes his urgent message isn't getting through to you, he will use more forceful behavior in an attempt to get you to care about what's bothering him. He might yell, use strong language, or get in your face to force you to acknowledge how upset he is.

If you give an angry person your "ears," she will usually lower her voice and become more rational because she no longer needs to resort to histrionics to get you to notice her. As English mathematician and physicist Sir Isaac Newton noted, "If I have ever made any valuable discoveries, it has been owing more to patient attention, than to any other talent." Patient attention can help you discover the real reasons behind someone's animosity, and you'll be halfway to erasing it.

Dedicate yourself to getting good at this skill, and you can improve every relationship you have. You will be a better supervisor, parent, employee, spouse, sibling, and friend. Remember how you feel about that person who really listens to you? Aren't you grateful for his or her presence in your life? Commit to doing this for other people, and they will hold you in the same high regard.

CARELESS LISTENING CAUSES CONFLICTS

"Conversation in the United States is a competitive exercise in which the first person to draw a breath is considered the listener."
—NATHAN MILLER

As Nathan Miller points out, most people don't listen, they just wait for their turn to talk. Yet putting your thoughts on hold for a moment in order to hear the other person's side is difficult when you feel something so intensely you can't wait to express it. It may feel like the other person is getting in the way of what you want to say.

My husband, a former naval aviator, calls this being "stuck on transmit." It's mechanically impossible for pilots to send and receive a radio transmission at the same time. They must talk, then listen.

You can use this image of a two-way radio to achieve two-way communication in your everyday conversations. The word *listen* contains the same letters as the word *silent* for good reason. Imagine yourself pressing an over-and-out button when you finish talking, and then giving your mind over to the incoming message. Silently absorb every word. Only after the other party has signed off do you sign on and respond to what's been said.

ACTIVATE YOUR INTEREST WITH THE THREE L'S

"It is easier to act yourself into feeling, than to feel yourself into acting."
—WILLIAM JAMES

Would you like to know a more tangible way to override this urge to value what you want to say more than what someone else wants to say? The secret is not to wait until you *feel* like listening to the other person. Face it, you may never want to hear his or her perspective. You've heard the expression "Listen up"? You can learn to activate your interest by listening up with the Three L's.

- **Look** at the other person. M. Scott Peck says, "You cannot truly listen to anyone and do anything else at the same time." Put down or turn away from what you're working on. Place your papers and pen on the desk. These body movements say, "This can wait. You are more important." Such actions on your part indicate, physically and psychologically, that he is your top priority.

- **Lift** your eyebrows, establish eye contact, and put an expression of interest on your face. If your face is slack, your level of interest will be the same. If your eyes wander, your mind will too. The simple act of focusing on the other person's face and raising your eyebrows counteracts lethargy and activates your curiosity.

- **Lean** forward and adopt an attentive posture so you're (literally and figuratively) on the edge of your seat. By leaning slightly toward him, you have just said with your body language, "I am here for you." He won't want or need to yell at you because you're so obviously extending yourself. By reaching out to the other person, you have made it difficult for him to be difficult.

LEARN TO LISTEN, LISTEN TO LEARN

"If you're not listening, you're not learning."
—LYNDON BAINES JOHNSON

After one program a participant came up to me and said, "I never realized how much my body language was alienating my employees. I've always prided myself on having an open-door policy. I didn't realize until today that my door might have been open, but my mind has been closed.

"When my employees want to talk with me, I'm often in the middle of something. Without realizing it, I've been treating them as an unwelcome interruption. I'll look up from what I'm doing and ask rather impatiently, 'Yes?' My abrupt manner translates to 'You're bothering me. Hurry up and let me get back to work.'

"When I return to the office, I'm going to schedule Listening Hours between ten and eleven and three and four so I'm not distractedly trying to field questions throughout the day while juggling urgent demands and deadlines. During those designated hours, I'll put everything else aside and make my employees and their concerns my first priority."

I complimented the woman for vowing to be more mindful of her staff and told her about a survey that asked employees from a wide variety of industries this one question: "Do you like your boss?" The results were surprising. Respondents who replied, "Yes, I like my boss," said the number one reason why was "He/she listens to me." Guess what reason was most frequently given for *not* liking your boss? "He/she doesn't listen to me."

In his funny book *Down Time,* Ron Dentinger quips: "My wife used to talk to herself. Well, she thought I was listening." In real life, people know when you're not listening. They will sense that you are distracted and interpret this as a lack of interest. Often they will stop trying to communicate because they've concluded that there's no point to it.

This wise manager understood if she didn't set aside time to listen to her employees, they would soon feel ignored, morale would suffer, and crucial issues would go unaddressed. She was smart to welcome their feedback with "open ears" so she could learn what wasn't working and take steps to correct it. As the saying goes, "If we don't have time to do it right the first time, when are we going to have time to do it over again?" By paying attention up front, she's going to avoid having to spend massive amounts of time to resolve situations that had escalated because she didn't invest the time at the outset to listen up.

DOMINATION VS. DOMINION

"If you want to lift yourself up, lift up someone else."
—BOOKER T. WASHINGTON

A modification of Washington's idea is, if you want to lift someone up, lower yourself. A schoolteacher said, "If you want children to believe you're really listening to them, kneel down. If they have to look up at you, they'll be reluctant to share their innermost thoughts because it's threatening to reveal yourself to someone who towers over you. They'll never believe you understand how they feel, because you're literally and figuratively not on their level. If you hunker down so you can see things eye to eye, they'll share more freely because they'll know intuitively you're seeing things from their perspective."

Perhaps you've been in the unnerving position of chairing a meeting and asking for discussion, only to be met with silence. If you are standing up and everyone else is seated, you may have unwittingly set up a "me boss, you peons" atmosphere. Standing over people denotes domination. (Dominate is interestingly defined as "to overlook from a superior elevation or command because of superior height or position.") Those seated may be intimidated by your position and not feel free to speak up.

If you want to encourage dialogue, sit down. Participants will be more comfortable contributing their opinions because you will have established a level playing field. Group members will be more likely to take an active role and listen to each other because the roles have been equalized. You will have established détente, "the relaxation of strained relations or tension."

Who is overdue for some listening from you? Who has received more than his share of "Not now," "Keep it short," "Hurry up," "Catch you later?" When are you going to see that person next? Vow right now to give him five minutes of your undivided attention. Put everything else out of your mind and make him the most important thing in your world for those few moments. Use the Three L's (Look, Lift, Lean) to preclude preoccupation. Concentrating on him is an eloquent way to say "I value you" and can compensate for other times when you're distracted and listening with half an ear.

ACTION PLAN FOR LISTENING UP!

Your friend has invited you to lunch to help him celebrate his promotion. Over your meal, he's excitedly telling you all about his new responsibilities. Though you're glad for him, you're scheduled for a performance evaluation that afternoon, and your mind keeps wandering. What do you do?

WORDS TO LOSE	WORDS TO USE
You continue to worry about how your performance evaluation is going to go. *"I wonder what my boss is going to say about that project report. What if I don't get that bonus I've been counting on?"*	You tell yourself that your friend is important to you and that he deserves your full focus. *"I can think about my performance appraisal when I get back to the office. For the next half-hour, I'm going to give Max my undivided attention."*
You grow increasingly restless and start fidgeting. *"I never should have agreed to this lunch in the first place."*	You activate your interest with the Three L's. *"I'm going to sit up, lean across the table, and lift my eyebrows so I'll feel more like listening."*
Your eyes wander and you notice several fellow employees walk in. *"I wonder how their appraisals went. Uh-oh, they don't look too happy."*	You keep your eyes on Max's face so your mind doesn't wander. *"I'm glad to hear Max got this new position. He deserves it."*

· Chapter 17 ·
Rules for Unruly Behavior

What would it be like to be driving along in your car only to discover that suddenly all the lines on the road, the traffic lights, the
crosswalks, and the signs indicating the right of way had disappeared?

It would be chaos, wouldn't it? No one would be safe.

Most human activities have rules. The rules of the road ensure
that you can pass within feet of cars speeding in the opposite direction—and feel no fear because you have faith other drivers will
obey the laws.

Every sport has rules. In football, you can't sack a quarterback
after he releases the ball. You're not allowed to curse a referee. Even
boxing has rules: you can't rabbit-punch, hit your opponent after
the bell rings, or land a blow below the belt.

Yet, surprisingly, most communication ("a process by which information is exchanged between individuals through a common system of symbols, signs, or behavior") doesn't have rules. There are
no agreed-upon guidelines to dictate what's appropriate and what's
not. Anything goes. People interrupt each other, monopolize conversations, and make personal attacks. With no standards of behavior established, individuals, as Michener notes, "run amok."

COMMUNICATION GUIDELINES

"Reality was such a jungle—with no signposts, landmarks, or boundaries."
—HELEN HAYES IN *REFLECTION: AN AUTOBIOGRAPHY*

One way to make sure that those beginning a long-term relationship can coexist comfortably and safely is to outline and agree upon communication guidelines right at the start. Meet with your partner, roommate, or family members and agree about what's permitted and what's not. Maybe you have terrible memories of your parents' sniping at each other in public, and you promise not to do that to each other. Perhaps you would like to institute your own more helpful variation of Phyllis Diller's advice: "Don't go to bed mad. Stay up and fight!" I'll always remember the time I suggested a good ground rule for marriage was "We will not threaten divorce during an argument." A woman in the audience clapped her hand to her forehead, exclaiming, "Too late!"

Karen Waggoner, the vice president of my speaking business, Action Seminars, has posted one rule in her house: there is to be no name-calling . . . and that includes "stupid," "jerk" and "dummy." Agree not to bring up old baggage that's already been apologized for. Agree upon a signal ("Ouch!" or "Time out!") to let someone know he's treading on thin ice and it's prudent to back off. By establishing communication covenants, you can maintain goodwill with and between your loved ones.

KEEP THE PEACE

"If they want peace, nations should avoid the pinpricks that precede cannon shots."
—NAPOLEON BONAPARTE

Over 11 million meetings take place in the United States every day. This is not a particularly alarming statistic, except that participants say over half their time spent in meetings is wasted (as revealed in a 1986 survey taken by the national firm Accountemps). Out-of-control meetings often do more damage than good by pitting people against each other and provoking divisiveness rather than co-operation.

These simple guidelines can help the chairperson successfully facilitate meetings so they don't deteriorate into brawls. By enforcing these ground rules, you can avoid the petty pinpricks that can escalate into out-and-out verbal warfare.

1. *One person speaks at a time.* If someone interrupts or if a couple of people start a side conversation, enforce this rule with these methods:

   - Look at the original speaker, hold your hand up toward them, and say in a firm yet warm voice, "Excuse me, [name of speaker], let's wait until we have everyone's attention." Be sure to finish your statement with a downward inflection. If your voice goes up at the end, you will sound whiny and tentative, and the interrupter will not feel compelled to cooperate.
   - Do not look at the interrupter. If you look at him, so will everyone else. The interrupter will feel embarrassed and will resent you for causing him to lose face in front of his peers.
   - If the interrupter continues talking, continue to look at the speaker and repeat your call to order in a louder, more commanding voice.
   - Only after everyone is silent do you give the floor back to the speaker with a flourish of your hand and a "Thank you, [name of speaker], please proceed. You were telling us about. . . ."

Having facilitated retreats and conferences for years, I can promise if you enforce this rule immediately and consistently early in a meeting, you will establish a positive precedent that carries throughout the discussion. Honoring the speaker's right to be heard will be the norm, and people will pay attention to each other and behave courteously instead of thoughtlessly barging in whenever they have something to say.

2. Participants can speak only once on each agenda item until everyone who wants to contribute has a chance to do so. This rule prevents forceful personalities from taking over the discussion and turning it into a diatribe while shy participants hold back because they're uncomfortable wresting the conversational ball from opinionated peers.

   How do you enforce this? If Mary speaks out of turn (before other group members have had a chance to offer their comments), put your palm up toward Mary and say, "Mary, we want to hear what you have to say, and first let's find out what the rest of the group thinks about this. Bob?"

   Be sure to practice Words to Use. The goal is to hold participants accountable, not to embarrass them. Instead of, "Mary, you'll have to wait until everyone else has a chance," or "Mary, I know you have strong feelings about this, but several other people . . . ," say, "Mary, you're welcome to respond as soon as everyone else has an opportunity to give their thoughts."

3. You can speak for up to two minutes (or substitute your own reasonable time limit) at a time. While this may seem unnecessarily strict, it serves an important purpose. My mom taught me, "That which can be done at any time rarely gets done at all." Unless there's a time limit, people have no reason to speak succinctly. They will repeat themselves, ramble, and wax eloquent (or not so eloquent) while the rest of the group goes to Tahiti in their minds.

   In their classic book, *Elements of Style,* Strunk and White say, "Vigorous writing is concise." Vigorous speaking is also concise. A two-minute maximum can transform boring bull sessions into fast-paced, productive meetings.

   Enforce this by appointing a group member as

timekeeper. They are to give a ten-second "warning." When time is up, gently and firmly interrupt and say, "Thanks, Brad, for that suggestion. Who else has an idea?"

BE PLEASANTLY UNPLEASANT

"Where laws end, tyranny begins."
—WILLIAM PITT, EARL OF CHATHAM

Our state Department of Education asked me to chair its annual conference. This event brings together students, teachers, administrators, parents, and DOE officials to discuss issues facing public schools.

The agenda included several emotionally charged issues, including mainstreaming of special education students, minimum grade-point averages required for participation in sports, and mandatory drug and sex education. At the end of the day, participants gave each other a standing ovation. They unanimously agreed the issues had been thoroughly addressed and that everyone had an equal opportunity to air his or her views. While specific individual suggestions may not have carried the day, the participants felt the process was fair, consensus had been reached, and they could support the outcome.

Why were we able to achieve a successful retreat when in the past this annual conference had consistently deteriorated into a shouting match? Because each focus group was facilitated by a trained mediator who outlined the ground rules at the start of the session and made sure everyone observed them. One of the mediators approached me afterward and said, "I just received the ultimate compliment. Our most opinionated participant stopped on his way out the door, shook my hand, praised me for keeping the session on track, and pronounced, 'You were pleasantly unpleasant.' "

I've always liked that characterization. A chairperson may need to be "pleasantly unpleasant" when administering these ground rules. It isn't always easy to grab the floor from a speaker who's ardently expounding a viewpoint. Stopping a heated discussion to suggest the focus be moved to action plans may initially ruffle some feathers, yet the result is worth it. Invariably, group members feel everyone's rights were honored rather than those of just a few aggressive individuals.

RESPECT EACH OTHER'S RIGHTS

"Between people, as among nations, respect of each other's rights ensures the peace." —BENITO JUAREZ

Three additional rules can ensure peaceful deliberation of even the most volatile subjects.

- *Negating other people's opinions is not allowed.* It's not permissible to say, "That's not how it happened" or "That's not true." Telling someone he's wrong is a surefire way to make him angry. Diplomatically disagree by using "I" statements: "I don't agree with that" or "I have a different impression of what happened." See the difference? Using the word *I* is a way to state your position without personally attacking a person with an opposing view.

- *Voices need to be kept down.* No shouting is allowed. This rule may seem petty, but it is the key to keeping a discussion reasonable. Stanley Horowitz has observed, "Nothing lowers the level of conversation more than raising the voice." He's right. The louder people talk, the less they listen. Speaking in a normal tone helps people interact objectively.

- *Focus on the future, instead of dwelling on the past.* This very important concept, already discussed in Chapters 9 and 11, bears repeating. Instead of spending time lamenting what should have been done (and why it wasn't), move on to what action can be taken and how this situation can be handled more effectively from now on.

LAY DOWN THE LAW

"If men were angels, no government would be necessary."
—JAMES MADISON

If people could be counted on to treat each other courteously, no regulations would be necessary. Unfortunately, most groups have at least one insensitive soul who if left to his own devices would thoughtlessly trample the rights of others. That's why it's necessary to lay down the law so participants are protected.

A friend of mine who lives in a forty-story apartment building called me with a success story. He reported, "Our annual condominium association meetings had become a nightmare. Some residents refused to go to them, for good reason. Last year the board president completely lost control. He actually ended up standing on his chair, banging his gavel and yelling for order. Neighbors were shouting at neighbors, people were walking out in disgust. It was a debacle.

"After reading your Tongue Fu! newsletter, I realized it didn't have to be like that, so I proposed we hire an impartial mediator to chair the proceedings. The board voted for it, and as a result, our meeting ran smoothly and without incident.

"The facilitator welcomed us, asked for introductions to set a friendly precedent, clarified the ground rules and agenda, and then kept the discussion moving forward instead of letting it bog down in personalities. The whole thing was over in two hours, instead of the five it took last year. If anyone started getting out of line, the mediator would simply point to the posted ground rules and then help him focus on issues rather than individuals. That one meeting reversed the negative spiral started by last year's disgrace and reestablished an amicable esprit de corps in our building."

ACTION PLAN FOR RULES FOR UNRULY BEHAVIOR

You are chairing a PTA meeting that you know in advance will be volatile because the school has announced it's canceling graduation ceremonies due to lack of funds. How do you manage the meeting?

WORDS TO LOSE

You begin by introducing the principal, who explains the decision.
"I want to bring Mr. Sato up so he can tell you why the graduation program has been canceled."

The principal is rudely interrupted and shouted down by an angry parent.
"You're out of line. Sit down and wait your turn like everybody else."

Several parents start talking among themselves and you suffer in silence.
"These people are so rude. They should give the poor guy a chance."

WORDS TO USE

You open the meeting by welcoming people and establishing ground rules.
"We're glad you're here tonight. Let's agree to some ground rules so we can discuss this important issue fairly."

You refer to the ground rules and hold the participant accountable for courtesy.
"Sir, you'll have a chance to contribute, and first, let's let Mr. Sato finish."

You put your hand up and ask the speaker to wait until everyone is quiet.
"Excuse me, Mr. Sato. Let's wait until we have everyone's attention . . ."

· Chapter 18 ·
Defuse Disputes

Would you like to know how to intervene diplomatically if you're forced to mediate a dispute?

Once while I was presenting a Tongue Fu! workshop to the Honolulu police department, a savvy officer told the group his secret for calming couples embroiled in a domestic dispute. He said when he arrives upon the scene, the people involved are almost always distraught. They often have different versions of what happened and want to get their side heard first. Emotions are high and tempers are short.

The officer said, "I've found the best thing I can do when people are at each other's throats is to take notes. I pull out my notepad and say these magical words: 'Each of you will get your turn. Now, ma'am (or sir), start at the beginning and tell me what happened.' "

RANT AND RAVE VS. REPORT

"Discussion is an exchange of knowledge; argument an exchange of emotion."
—ROBERT QUILLEN

The officer continued, "Nothing positive can be accomplished when people are shouting at each other. Chronicling what happened from the beginning forces the disputants to stop, slow down, and reconstruct the chain of events. Instead of ranting and raving, they're reporting. It moves hotheads from an emotional to a logical frame of mind.

"Having someone else write down their foul language also makes people aware of how their profanity will sound to others. They realize it's not in their best interest to have a record of their off-color remarks, so they're motivated to stop swearing.

"Note taking also keeps people from rambling or saying the same thing over and over. If they start rehashing something for the third time, I say, 'I've got that right here . . . and then what happened?' And finally, after I've logged it all down, I read back what they've said so each is satisfied their version of the story has been heard accurately."

DON'T PUT UP WITH PUT-DOWNS

"Rudeness is the weak man's imitation of strength." —ERIC HOFFER

A woman in one of my workshops said her attorney recommended she take notes whenever her former partner tried to intimidate her. "My ex-husband was a very abusive man. I always felt like I was walking on eggshells because I never knew what was going to set him off. If I tried to defend myself, he would become more aggressive until I would give in and go along with what he wanted.

"My lawyer suggested I carry pen and paper with me and write down what he was saying. The next time my former husband started in on me, I got out my notebook. He demanded to know, 'What the %#$@ do you think you're doing?' I calmly replied, 'I'm writing down what you're saying.' 'Why the %$#@ are you doing that?' 'Why do you think?' I answered, and that was that. My ex realized these transcripts of his outbursts could be used as evidence against him in court, so he no longer unleashes his rage on me."

This woman is indeed in an extreme situation, but her story does illustrate the usefulness of recording what's being said. Taking notes doesn't have to be done for punitive reasons. It simply makes people aware that "what you're saying can and will be used against you," so they are motivated to speak courteously rather than cruelly.

I had a chance to use this technique recently at the airport. I had pulled over and engaged my emergency blinkers to indicate I was loading the van when an obviously irritated security officer walked over, banged on my windshield with her fist, and yelled, "Move this %$#@ car away from the curb. You can't stop here." I was about to explain that my husband was coming out with several large suitcases when she rolled her eyes in exasperation and said disgustedly, "Stupid! Can't you read signs?"

Now, I know her patience was stretched to the limit by the stressful conditions, but there was no excuse for her to use that kind of language or that tone of voice. At first I was shocked, and then I reached over to my purse, got out a pen and piece of paper, and said politely yet pointedly, "Excuse me, what was that you said?" Our eyes met. She realized she didn't want this example of poor customer service reported to her supervisor and that she had clearly been in the wrong. Her expression changed. She said, "Please clear this lane as soon as you're loaded up," and walked on.

DOCUMENT DIFFICULT BEHAVIOR

"Action is the antidote to despair."   —JOAN BAEZ

A variation on Joan Baez's quote might be that documentation is the antidote to disrespect. A personnel manager at one of my workshops confirmed the importance of logging illegal or inappropriate behavior. She said, "If an employee complains to me about someone, it's difficult to take action unless the date, time, and exact nature of the offending behavior have been documented. If you work with someone who is treating customers or coworkers improperly, don't just tell your supervisor about it. That's too subjective, because it's your word against theirs. Substantiate your claims by writing down what was said when and to whom so your manager has tangible evidence to investigate."

A teacher in the same session agreed. "I used to call parents at home to tell them when their child had misbehaved. They would often defend their child and get angry with me for picking on their kid. Now, if one of my students acts up, I detail what happened in a note and send it home with them. The note is an objective account of what took place, and the parents are more likely to focus on the facts instead of looking for a fight with me."

ACTION PLAN FOR DEFUSING DISPUTES

You're driving along when you come upon an accident involving two vehicles. You slow down to see if anyone needs assistance and see that the two people involved are neighbors of yours. They are yelling obscenities at each other. You quickly get out of your car to intervene so their shouting match doesn't come to blows. How do you handle this situation?

WORDS TO LOSE	WORDS TO USE
You try to calm them down by appealing to their reason. *"Hey, you two, cut this out. Yelling at each other is only going to make things worse."*	You stop their ranting and raving by taking notes. *"Each of you will get your turn. Now, Carl, start at the beginning and tell me . . ."*
They continue blaming and cursing at each other. *"Would the two of you shut the %$#@ up! Swearing is going to make things worse."*	You ask them to clarify what they've said to make them aware they don't want a record of their hostile comments. *"Dan, what was that you said again? I want to make sure I have it down right."*
Your neighbors keep saying the same thing over and over, getting louder with each repetition. *"Carl, that's the tenth time you said it was Dan's fault."*	You use your notes to keep them from repeating the same information again and again. *"Okay, I've got that right here . . . and then what happened?"*

· Chapter 19 ·

Approach with an Open Mind

Do you know someone so obnoxious that the mere sight of him is enough to make you turn tail and head in the other direction (Run Fu!)? Are there certain disagreeable people in your life, and the mere mention of their name is enough to conjure up a negative image?

The following example shows what happens when people prejudge others. Upon receiving an honorary award at the Academy Awards one year, Sir Laurence Olivier gave an eloquent acceptance speech. At least many of the people in the audience *thought* it was eloquent. The TV cameras showed many teary-eyed people in the crowd, moved by Olivier's words.

Afterward, the next award recipient Jon Voight complimented Olivier on his speech. Olivier demurred and said his talk hadn't made much sense; he had forgotten what he was going to say. A disbelieving Voight argued that the presentation had been brilliant. Only when they replayed his remarks on the video monitor did Voight finally see for himself that the speech had been less than perfect.

How could this have happened? If Voight and the audience had really been listening, they would have been scratching their heads and wondering what he was talking about. However, they weren't listening. They had prejudged Olivier and had become mesmerized by his style.

WITHHOLD JUDGMENT

"A great many people think they are thinking when they are merely rearranging prejudices."　　　　　　　　—WILLIAM JAMES

This may be one of the most difficult aspects of communication—to overcome one's natural proclivity to judge people based on appearance, their manner, one's experience of them, and any preconceptions one has about this type of person. As the story about Olivier illustrates, when people allow themselves to be swayed by the personality (positive or negative) of whoever is talking, they stop paying attention to what that person is actually saying. Benjamin Franklin wisely concluded, "He that would live in peace and at ease must not speak all he knows, nor judge all he sees."

One supervisor admitted he had fallen into the judgment trap. He said, "I'm guilty. I've labeled my employees the Troublemaker, the Problem Child, the Whiner, the Witch. If the Troublemaker walks into my office, I'm already prepared for a fight. If there's a phone message from the Problem Child, I'm already steeling myself for a catastrophe. I can see that it is not fair to write them off this way, but I didn't make up those nicknames out of the blue, they deserve them. How can I ignore repeated behavior?"

GIVE 'EM A CHANCE

"He that never changes his opinions, never corrects his mistakes, and will never be wiser on the morrow than he is today."
　　　　—TYRONE EDWARDS, AMERICAN AUTHOR AND COMPILER
　　　　　　　　OF *THE NEW DICTIONARY OF THOUGHTS*

Edna Ferber contributed a variation on this theme when she said, "A closed mind is a dying mind." Approach each situation with an open rather than a closed mind by reminding yourself that you can't know what someone's going to say until after she's finished talking. Wait until she has said her piece before passing judgment.

How do you manage this? Keep in mind these four words: "Give them a chance." If you find yourself shutting someone off because you don't like him or her, use this four-word phrase to help form *accurate* rather than *erroneous* conclusions about this person.

Instead of mentally dismissing troublemakers, listen with an open mind. They may surprise you and behave in an unexpected way. If you hadn't given them a chance, you wouldn't have registered this different behavior. If the Whiner does indeed whine, then at least you can respond to his comments based on their intrinsic merit rather than rejecting any ideas the person might have outright.

A woman in one of my workshops spoke up plaintively: "I know this makes sense, but I've been married to the same man for twenty-five years. How *many* chances are we supposed to give 'em?" Everyone laughed, and she went on to say, "When my husband comes home from work, I usually ask about his day. Ten seconds later, I'm thinking, 'Here we go again . . .' or 'I've heard this before.' "

I'm not going to "pull a Pollyanna" and suggest that you give people a chance ad infinitum. The truth is, this woman probably *has* heard her husband's litany of complaints before. She has to ask herself if on this specific occasion she can and should muster enough interest and energy to listen to him with renewed interest. Some days she should, some days she shouldn't. Some days she might be too burned out herself to listen to the latest in a long line of work-related insults. Other days he may seem particularly down and she might choose to give him a sympathetic ear. She could fast-forward through her impatience and supply the incentive to listen to it one more time by asking herself, "How would I feel?"

UNLOCK YOUR LABELS

"The more one judges, the less one loves."   —HONORÉ DE BALZAC

A teacher once told me she was going to post this quote from Balzac on the bulletin board above her desk. "I've got twenty-five kids in my class this year and I really did a disservice to one my of students. Joey frequently interrupts, teases the other children, hardly ever finishes his projects, and rarely listens. I used to resent him for taking up so much of my time.

"Then, at one of our Wednesday afternoon teacher meetings, our school nurse showed a movie explaining what it's like to have attention deficit hyperactivity disorder (ADHD). The film was made from the perspective of someone who is hyperactive, and for the first time I understood Joey's 'world.' I finally realized what it must be like to be in his skin—to have so much energy you literally can't sit still. I learned that he is so super-sensitive to his environment, it's like being bombarded by a perpetual onslaught of sights and sounds. When I experienced six hours of school through his eyes . . . well, suffice it to say, I saw him in a different light. I relabeled his disruptive behavior as hormonal rather than hostile, and it's helped me be more accepting of him."

LOVE VS. LABEL

"Tolerance is the positive and cordial effort to understand another's beliefs, practices, and habits without necessarily sharing or accepting them."
—JOSHUA LIEBMAN

Ethnic stereotypes are particularly toxic because those who are prejudiced distort everything they hear to fit into and provide support for their biases. According to Karl Menninger, "Fears are educated into us, and can, if we wish, be educated out of us." If you know that during your childhood, prejudices were educated into you, you can, if you want, educate them out of you. Actively listen to what each person says and draw conclusions based on what the individual says, rather than on dated attitudes and hasty first impressions.

A young woman once told this poignant story. "I moved from a farm community to a big college town to attend our state university. When my dorm roommate discovered I was from the boondocks—her words—she decided to take me under her wing. She warned me about certain ethnic groups on campus and told me to avoid them. I had played clarinet in high school and was looking forward to trying out for the marching band, but she pigeonholed them as a bunch of losers.

"I was naive and didn't know any better, so I took her at her word. I figured she was a junior and knew a lot more than I did. I hung out with her crowd that first semester and was miserable. They were always putting people down, and it took me several months to realize their opinions said a lot more about them than they did about the people they were accusing of being uncool or unsafe.

"I finally got fed up with their narrow-minded attitudes and went my own way. I joined the band after semester break, and ended up traveling all over the country with them to compete in parades and do halftime shows at football games. The first-chair clarinetist, who was of the ethnic group my roommate had warned me about, became my best friend, and we still keep in touch. I can't imagine what those four years would have been like if I had continued to buy into their bigoted beliefs. I learned a very important lesson. I make up my own mind about people, instead of letting other people make it up for me."

"The worst prison would be a closed heart," observes Pope John Paul II. Prison is defined as "a state of confinement or captivity." Are there people in your life you've written off because others have told you they're no good? Is that fair? How can you conclude someone has no value when you do not know him or her? Don't close your mind and heart to people by hanging on to stereotypes and prejudices. If your goal is to love rather than label people, give them a chance.

ACTION PLAN FOR APPROACHING WITH AN OPEN MIND

Your sixty-year-old widowed father has remarried and you're about to meet your new stepmother. Your sister has already met your dad's new bride and doesn't like her. She says the woman is very possessive and clingy. How do you approach this first meeting?

WORDS TO LOSE	WORDS TO USE
With no direct experience of the woman, you adopt your sister's opinion. *"Why did Dad have to marry someone like her anyway?"*	You decide it's not fair to write your stepmother off when you haven't even met. *"I'll hold off making any judgments until we've spent some time together."*
The first thing you notice is that she's holding on to your father's arm like she's never going to let go. *"Looks like Sis was right. Look at that death grip she's got on Dad."*	You approach them and greet warmly the woman your father has chosen to wed. *"I'm going to give her a chance. I won't know what she's like until after I get to know her."*
You continue to fit everything she says and does into your preconceptions. *"Why did Dad choose this woman? She's going to keep him under lock and key."*	You keep an open mind so you can draw conclusions based on merit. *"They look very happy together. I'm glad Dad found someone who so obviously loves him."*

· Chapter 20 ·

Share Control

Would you like to know how to transcend struggles for control?

A wise taxi driver was the first to introduce me to the concept of sharing rather than taking control. I was late wrapping up a workshop in Waikiki and had less than an hour to catch my plane back to Maui. I hailed a cab and quickly explained my plight. The cabby had obviously been around the block a few times and knew better than to set himself up for failure. He turned to me and asked respectfully, "We can take the freeway or Nimitz Highway. Which do you prefer?"

I deferred to him. "Whichever is fastest, please." He shook his head politely and said, "You choose." I picked one and we started on our way. I wondered why he'd wanted me to make the decision, so I asked him about it.

He explained: "I've learned that when people are in a hurry, it's a mistake for me to select the route. If we get tied up in traffic and my fare's late, they feel it's my fault and get angry at me. If the passenger chooses how to get there and for some reason we don't make it on time, then they take the responsibility rather than blaming me."

POSE OPTIONS AND LET THEM DECIDE

*"Whether or not we support a solution depends a lot on whether it's being
done to us—or by us."* —TONGUE FU'ISM

From this day forward, if you're facing a tough decision involving
others, don't unilaterally arrive at the action to be taken and present it as a fait accompli. If you do, even if it's the only option, the
people affected will resist. Why? Because it's being done *to* them
and not *by* them.

Instead, think of two equally acceptable alternatives, present
both to the group, and let them choose. The people involved will
be a lot happier with the decision because they made it.

Remember this technique if you deal with the public in your job.
Instead of telling customers what to do, give them two options and
ask which they'd prefer. Instead of saying, "We don't have an appointment available until next Monday at one," say, "We can
schedule your visit Monday at one or three. Which works best for
you?" Instead of "We'll have to refund your money because the
concert has been canceled," ask, "Would you like a refund, or
would you prefer credit toward our fall concert series?" Giving people the opportunity to make a choice puts them in charge of their
experience and will dramatically increase their satisfaction with the
interaction.

MAKE OTHERS PART OF THE PROCESS

*"People are usually more convinced by reasons they discovered themselves
than by those found by others."* —BLAISE PASCAL

A seminar group was discussing this issue of control. One man
seemed particularly fascinated with the insight that even when
you're acting in the best interests of the group, they may not appreciate your leadership because they feel left out. They'll probably drag their feet because they haven't had a chance to contribute
to the decision-making process.

He said, "I wish I had known this last year. My oldest son was going away to college in the fall, and I realized if we were ever going to take that driving vacation we had always talked about, it was going to have to be that summer. I called AAA to get maps and spent hours studying all the possible routes across America, designing our itinerary, and making reservations.

"The big day finally came. We picked up our motor home in California and started driving. We hadn't gone ten miles when my youngest daughter asked, 'So, Dad, when are we getting to Disneyland?' I explained we weren't because it was too crowded in July and not worth waiting in long lines.

"She couldn't believe it. 'We're half an hour away from Disneyland, and we're not going?' I explained that we had to get to the Grand Canyon in two days, so we had a lot of driving to get under our belts. Suffice it to say, she wasn't very pleased with this decision and grumbled about it for the rest of the day."

He continued: "Have any of you ever driven east out of Los Angeles? All you can see from horizon to horizon is hot, dry desert with heat waves shimmering up from the melting asphalt. We couldn't wait to get to our campground so we could cool off and play in their swimming pool. We arrived after twelve hours of driving, hooked up the RV, and walked over to the pool with great anticipation . . . only to discover it had a cracked bottom and not one drop of water. *Argghh!*"

"We finally got to the Grand Canyon and couldn't find anywhere to park our large Winnebago. I drove around and around and finally gave up and left the darn thing on the side of the road. At that point, I didn't care if it got towed. They could have it!

"We walked over to the side of the canyon. My youngest daughter took one look at the Big Ditch and turned to me, wailing, 'We missed Disneyland for this?' "

ARE WE HAVING FUN YET?

"Everything is funny as long as it is happening to somebody else."
—WILL ROGERS

The father continued with his vacation vignette: "It went downhill from there. The next morning, all I heard were complaints from the backseat. 'Are we there yet?' 'How much longer?' I felt unappreciated and resentful. Didn't they know I had spent hours planning our vacation? Didn't they realize I took three weeks off work so we could have fun together? I finally grabbed my auto club map, ripped it in half, threw it in the air, and said, 'I give up. *You* plan the vacation.'

"And that's what we did. We divvied up the days. My daughter had a day, my son had a day, my wife had a day, and I had a day. On your day, you could do anything you wanted as long as you got to our destination by seven P.M. and kept within the agreed spending limit. If it was your day and you wanted to sleep in, everyone slept in. If we were driving along and you wanted to see a live snake show, we stopped and saw it.

"You know what? We had the best time together as a family we'd ever had. I belatedly realized why they weren't enjoying their vacation. It wasn't *their* vacation. It was *my* vacation."

I have retold this man's story many times, and it never fails to get a reaction. Many people have been there. One woman who reacted strongly to my rendition of this tale told me afterward: "That was our family. The same thing happened to us. Our father rented a motor home to drive through New England so we could see the fall foliage. Unfortunately for my dad, the van had a TV and Luke and Laura's wedding on *General Hospital* was infinitely more interesting to us than a bunch of trees. I'll always remember my dad roaring at us from the front seat, 'I did not pay two thousand bucks so you could watch soap operas. Now turn that thing off and get up here and *look at the leaves.*'"

Have you, like the parents in these stories, ever put a lot of time and effort into organizing something, and instead of gratitude, all you got was complaints? People will often be ungrateful if you're in control of the situation and they're not. If you can learn to share control instead of taking control, people will feel it's *their* vacation.

Being in charge of a situation doesn't mean your role is to make all decisions yourself. When resolving controversial issues, research the situation, outline fair guidelines, pose reasonable options, and let those affected decide. Some may not like the final outcome, but they'll be more willing to accept it because they were part of the process that helped produce it. They'll have found out for themselves that in that set of circumstances it was the best decision possible.

GIVE-AND-TAKE CONTROL

"Each of us seeks to remain on top in an encounter. If we succeed in outwitting the other person and our viewpoint prevails, then we feel strong rather than weak and we receive a psychological boost."
—JAMES REDFIELD, *THE CELESTINE PROPHECY*

In one-to-one relationships, watch out for this destructive desire to top the other person. Learn once and for all that any psychological boost you may get from winning at someone else's expense is purely temporary. As Odetta said, "The better we feel about ourselves, the fewer times we have to knock somebody else down to stand tall." The reverse is also true. The more times you choose to help someone up rather than knock them down, the better you'll feel about yourself.

View fellow human beings as cohorts rather than competitors. Instead of communicating in a classic top-down style, seek collaborative solutions. Instead of striving to outwit other people, dedicate yourself to generating win-win situations and resolutions. According to Bertrand Russell, "It's coexistence or no existence."

A stockbroker in one of my seminars spoke up: "I believe this, but the people around me sure don't. What you're talking about flies in the face of everything I was taught in business school about climbing the corporate ladder. The financial industry is extremely competitive. In my company, it's dog-eat-dog. If you don't produce, you're out on the street. We're all competing for the same clients and for the same promotions. You're almost forced to be like that guy Gordon Gecko in the movie *Wall Street:* "Greed is good.""

A woman at the same seminar spoke up. "I agree. What can we

do if someone else is trying to control us? What if we're trying to live win-win lives, but the people around us aren't operating with the same principles?"

Part IV of this book deals with these very issues, focusing on how you can continue to be kind and cooperative when others are being cruel and competitive and on how you can stand up for yourself and say no. You'll learn how to live a life of values even when those around you aren't.

ACTION PLAN FOR SHARING CONTROL

You and a friend head up to the mountains for a weekend of skiing. He's much better than you are and soon is ready for the more difficult slopes. You feel you need a lot more practice before you tackle the advanced runs but your friend pressures you to accompany him. How do you resolve this?

WORDS TO LOSE

You don't appreciate him taking charge of the situation.
"Mark, you're not going to pressure me into going down something I'm not ready for."

Mark insists that he'll watch out for you and says to stop being such a chicken.
"How can you say I don't have anything to worry about? Have you seen the size of those moguls up there?"

Your friend continues to see it as an either-or situation.
"Stop trying to force me to do something I'm not comfortable with. I didn't come all this way to spend the day fighting."

WORDS TO USE

You know you can work things out so you both win.
"Let's see if we can figure out how to work this so both of us can enjoy the skiing."

You seek a resolution that will allow both of you a measure of control.
"It's only fair you don't want to keep skiing the bunny hill, and it's fair that I don't want to risk breaking a leg."

You pose a couple of options that let both of you get what you want.
"How about if you explore the Black Diamond slopes and I'll practice on the easier runs? We can swap notes at lunch."

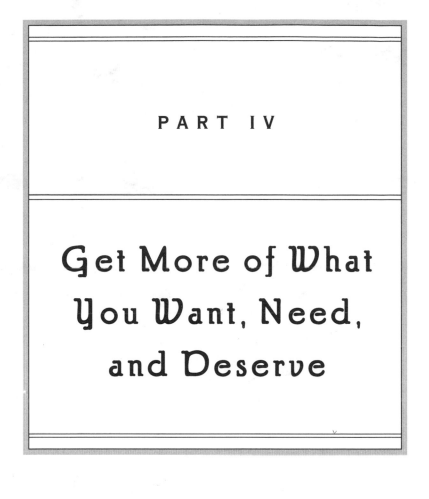

PART IV

Get More of What
You Want, Need,
and Deserve

· Chapter 21 ·

Choose Your Battles

How can you determine when something is sufficiently significant to warrant being brought out into the open? How can you know when to hold 'em and when to fold 'em?

To confront or not to confront, that is the question. Just because you don't like how someone is treating you doesn't mean it's smart to speak up just then. What *is* smart is to consider all the possible consequences *before* you confront someone.

Therese, a friend of mine and director of patient care for a large medical group, finally succeeded in getting pregnant when she was forty years old. She had a difficult nine months and spent the last trimester at home. She gave birth to a healthy son, but she needed more time to recover fully before she could return to work. Her employer was generous with the maternity leave, held her position open, and paid her her full salary for the months she was not at work.

Shortly after she resumed her duties, Therese learned by accident that her salary was almost $10,000 a year less than those of the other department heads. She felt this discrepancy was grossly unfair because her credentials, responsibilities, and seniority were the equivalent of those of her peers. I happened to be visiting her right after she found out this disturbing fact. She was determined to talk to her CEO the next day and demand that this inequity be rectified.

I asked her one question: "Therese, is it good timing?"

When she thought about the situation from that perspective, she realized that her employer had made major concessions to her over the last few months. If she marched into his office with an attitude about her compensation, her boss wouldn't be in a mood to agree to a pay raise. He'd probably be in a mood to say, "You're more trouble than you're worth."

She realized that instead of getting angry about this, she should prove her worth to the company through several months of stellar work performance. If she approached the CEO about this issue after she had reestablished her value to the company, he'd be much more likely to consider her request in a favorable light.

CALCULATE THE RISKS

"God, give us grace to accept with serenity the things that cannot be changed, courage to change the things which should be changed, and the wisdom to distinguish the one from the other."

—REINHOLD NIEBUHR

Think of a person or a situation that is bothering you. Use these CYB (Choose Your Battles) criteria to figure out whether it's wise or risky to speak up. Ask yourself:

1. *Is it trivial?* Maybe a salesclerk called you honey, and you don't like being addressed this way. Ask yourself, "Am I ever going to see this person again?" Admittedly, this issue does not affect world peace. You can afford to let it roll off your back.

2. *Is it a persistent concern?* What if you're working with a salesclerk who's calling you honey twenty times a day? Now the stakes are higher. This is not a one-

time irritation. It may matter enough at this point to have a talk with the clerk.

3. *What's the history of the situation?* Evaluate the extenuating circumstances. Maybe this is your first week on the job, while the woman who calls you honey has been employed at the store for twenty years. Have you worn out your welcome by complaining about other issues recently? Do you have "goodwill credit," or is your account tapped out? Are other people bothered by this, or only you?

4. *Is the behavior intentional or innocent?* Do you think she's doing this on purpose to antagonize you, or is it meant as an affectionate endearment?

5. *Can or will it change?* Is the person capable of changing her behavior? Is she motivated to treat you differently? Maybe this woman *could* call you by your given name (after all, you wear a name tag), but she's been calling women honey her whole adult life and sees no reason to change now. Maybe her attitude is "This is the way I am. If you don't like it, tough!"

   I once saw some graffiti that advised, "Never try to teach a pig to sing. It's a waste of your time, and it annoys the pig." You may conclude that trying to get this person to stop calling people honey is the equivalent of teaching a pig to sing.

6. *Is it a short-term win and a long-term loss?* Ask yourself, "If I go to the mat over this issue, what will happen? Could I win the battle and lose the war? Would it be better to overlook this minor issue in favor of a larger goal?" General George S. Patton suggested, "Take calculated risks. This is quite different from being rash." Maybe the toll for crossing this particular bridge could be a strained working relationship, and you're not willing to pay the price.

PUT YOUR MIND IN GEAR
BEFORE YOU PUT YOUR MOUTH IN MOTION

"Only a fool tests the depth of the water with both feet."
—AFRICAN PROVERB

Running through the checklist can help you decide whether to speak now or forever hold your peace. After taking these factors into account and testing the water, you may decide the issue is too petty to pursue. Or you may decide you're not willing to turn the other cheek, and it's important enough to bring to the other person's attention. Either way, you'll be acting *with* thought, instead of putting your mouth in motion while your mind is in park.

A friend of mine uses these Choose Your Battles (CYB) criteria to handle a minor issue that had bothered him for years. He likes his full name, Robert, and used to smolder silently whenever strangers shortened it to Bob or Rob. Now, if someone takes it upon himself to call my friend by a nickname, he asks himself if he's ever going to see the person again. If not, Robert lets it go. If he is going to be spending time with the person, he simply states, "I prefer to be called Robert."

TO NAG OR NOT TO NAG

"In long-term relationships, we tend to overvalue what someone is not, and undervalue what they are." —ANONYMOUS

In Tongue Fu! workshops for couples, I ask participants to think of one thing they don't like about their spouse/partner. (A wiseacre once cracked, "Just one?") I then ask them to use the six criteria to evaluate that disturbing behavior so they can decide once and for all whether it's worth pursuing. If the undesirable trait is never going to change and their partner has other saving graces, maybe it's time to focus on all their partner is instead of all he or she is not.

One woman told me this idea saved her marriage. "My husband

loves to play golf. In fact he *lives* to play golf. Every Saturday, he's out there, rain or shine, with his buddies from seven A.M. to two P.M. He misses all our kids' athletic events. I'm always the one chauffeuring them around and trying to explain why he doesn't come watch them play.

"No matter how much I protested that this was hurting his children (and me!), golf was basically a nonnegotiable item for him. He felt he worked hard all week and deserved to have half a day to spend as he pleased. I had accumulated so much resentment over this, I had almost decided to give him an ultimatum: if golf was more important than his family, we'd be better off without him.

ULTIMATUM VS. UNDERSTANDING

"Most people don't wait for someone to drive them crazy. They drive themselves."
—ANONYMOUS

The golf widow said she went through each of the CYB criteria to decide whether or not to give him an ultimatum. "I realized he wasn't going to stop playing golf. He'd already told me flat out that golf keeps him sane, and that he intends to play until they have to prop him up to tee off.

"Then I asked myself the important question 'Is this issue worth jeopardizing our marriage?' I started thinking about all the things Austin *is* instead of this one thing he's not. I concluded, on balance, that this issue had grown out of proportion for me and that it was not worth tossing away a twenty-year relationship.

"I decided that instead of driving myself crazy over his hobby, I would change my attitude about it. Instead of getting mad, I would be glad he was skilled at a sport that gave him a chance to be outdoors with friends. I decided to help the kids focus on all the things their father did for them instead of this one thing he didn't. And I decided to meet my best friend on Sundays for a morning walk/talk so I wasn't getting shortchanged on weekends. I chose not to fight this losing battle, and as a result, we've all won."

SEEK NEW LANDSCAPES VS. SEE WITH NEW EYES

"Everyone thinks of changing the world, but no one thinks of changing himself."
—LEO TOLSTOY

Think of a situation you're unhappy with. There are basically three things you can do about it. You can:

1. *Change the other person.* This is hardly likely.

2. *Change the situation.* Before you take some drastic action (i.e., quit your job, get a divorce, or drop out of school), first ask yourself, "Is the change I'm contemplating a trade *up?*" If not, walking out is rash rather than wise. In your haste to get out of a situation that makes you unhappy, you may end up in another that leaves you equally miserable.

   As Dorothea Dix said, "So many persons who think divorce a panacea for every ill find out, when they try it, that the remedy is worse than the disease." In other words, make sure the grass on the other side of the fence really is greener before you hop over.

3. *Change yourself.* This is always an option, and it comes with good news. In the process of changing yourself (whether you become more assertive or whether you choose to focus your attention on the positive aspects of the relationship), you often influence how the other person treats you, which improves your circumstances. By changing yourself, you can change your world for the better.

"Instead of seeking new landscapes," Marcel Proust suggested, "develop new eyes." If the consequences for taking action are formidable, then it may be time to develop new eyes. Choosing to see your present landscape with a new perspective could improve your view.

ACTION PLAN FOR CHOOSING YOUR BATTLES

Your neighbors have a teenage son who loves to play rock and roll loudly. It's eleven o'clock at night and you're trying to get to sleep. You've had enough of the noise and are ready to call and say, "Turn off that blasted music." What do you do?

WORDS TO LOSE

You call without considering the consequences and tell your neighbor exactly how you feel. *"Do you know what time it is? Either you shut off that noise or I'm going to come over and do it myself."*

You continue to nag them about the disruptive music. *"How do you expect anyone to get any peace and quiet with that garbage blaring?"*

You issue a threat. *"I'm going to call the cops unless that stereo is turned off now."*

WORDS TO USE

You choose your battles. *"Is this a trivial matter? Is it a persistent concern? It may be petty, but it happens at least three nights a week."*

You continue to evaluate whether it's worth going to the mat over this issue. *"Are they doing it innocently or intentionally? Can or will it change? What's the history? Is it good timing?"*

You decide it's important enough to address. *"Jerry, could you ask your son to turn his music down, please."*

· Chapter 22 ·

Say No

Would you like to learn how to say no without risking your job and friendships? A big part of Tongue Fu! is learning to honor your rights and other's rights at the same time. This can be a challenge. When do you put other people first; when do you put yourself first?

If you constantly give in to and say yes to other people, your relationships will not be very healthy. Your relationships will be equally unhealthy if you consider only how you feel. **The key to creating and maintaining successful relationships is to keep the needs being met in balance.** This is easier said than done, so I've developed a tangible tool to help you clarify when it's appropriate to go along with what people want and say yea, and when it's appropriate to assert yourself and say nay.

If you're faced with a tough decision that is tearing you in half, visualize this old-fashioned scale. Identify the different needs being met and not met, and place them on the appropriate side.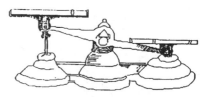
You now have an objective accounting of who's been taken care of and who hasn't. If the scale is tilted in your

favor, then maybe it's time to give the other person what he wants. If you've been consistently compromising your needs, then turning down this request is not selfish, it's smart.

SELFISH OR SELFLESS?

"Selfishness is not living as one wishes to live—it is always asking others to live as one wishes to live."
—OSCAR WILDE

Suppose someone is pleading with you to do something, and you feel pulled in two directions. Take a few minutes to fill out the scale. The completed figure can help you arrive at an answer you can live with. If it's obvious that you've been looking out for the other person's interests to the exclusion of yours, it's appropriate to say no. If the other person's wishes have been ignored lately, perhaps it's time to say yes.

A man named Glenn spoke up in one of my workshops and said he agreed with this concept in theory but had a hard time practicing it in real life. "I've always been like that character in the musical who sings, 'I can't say no.' You've heard the advice about giving assignments to the busiest people because you know the jobs will get done? That's me. I've got meetings almost every night of the week. I'm involved in so many organizations, I can hardly keep track of them. I'm running on empty, but every time I pledge to cut back, someone begs me to take on another project."

GLENN	OTHERS
☑ Family	☑ Rotary Club
☑ Health	☑ United Way
☑ Friends	☑ Alumni assoc.
☑ Hobbies	☑ Church council
	☑ PTA president
	☑ 4H advisor
	☑ Homeowners assoc.

The class adopted Glenn's situation as a class project. One attendee asked about his different obligations, while another jotted them down on the scale (see the diagram). Glenn obviously was serving many associations. How about his

own needs? How was his health? How were his relationships with his friends and family? Was he involved in any hobbies? Was he spending time the way he really wanted, or was his life spinning out of control?

Glenn said the long list of community commitments on one side of the scale as compared with the paltry list of personal activities on the other side settled this issue for him once and for all. He said, "When I tried to work this out in my mind, I just got confused. Thinking it through muddled it even more; putting it on paper clarified it. From now on, I'm going to use the scale so I can make informed decisions instead of just caving under the pressure of the moment and paying for it afterward."

SAY NO WITHOUT LOSING YOUR JOB, FRIENDS, OR FAMILY

"There are three possible broad approaches to the conduct of interpersonal relations. The first is to consider one's self only and ride roughshod over others. The second is always to put others before one's self. The third approach is the golden mean . . . the individual places himself first, and takes others into account."
—JOSEPH WOLPE

Glenn went on, "Now my dilemma is how to cut back on my heavy schedule without alienating my associates." Good point. How can you turn down requests without jeopardizing personal or professional relationships? You can say no without worry by using the following four steps.

1. *Say, "I'd like to have some time to think about it."* If you have a history of collapsing under pressure only to later lament, "What did I get myself into?" then vow you won't spontaneously agree to any additional time-consuming responsibilities. Negotiators know people make concessions they wouldn't ordinarily consent to when pressed to give an immediate an-

swer. Don't let yourself be caught off guard by mental strong-arm tactics. Give yourself privacy so you can clear-headedly evaluate the needs being met.

Note that I am not advocating avoidance. I am acknowledging that in the real world, becoming more assertive does not happen overnight. It's unrealistic to suggest that people can instantly stop being doormats if that's what they've been for years. This first step can ensure that you think twice before adding obligations so you no longer automatically cave under coercion.

2. *Say no and yes.* Turn down this particular request and suggest an alternative that's more on your terms. If Glenn was asked to be an officer of his professional association, he could beg off that particular labor-intensive position and offer to contribute in another way. Perhaps he could write a column for the club's monthly newsletter, a task he could do at home in his spare time that wouldn't require coordinating with other board members.

3. *Say no and solve the problem through other means.* Let them know you're not available and recommend someone who would do a good job. You can offer your expertise and help produce the desired results, even if you're not personally involved in the event itself.

4. *Say no graciously, firmly, and without guilt.* If you've been giving and never getting, you have the right to just say no without feeling bad about it. "I'm flattered by your offer, and I've promised to leave my evenings and weekends open for my family."

If people persist, employ Words to Use to keep the conversation constructive. Saying "I know you need volunteers to help run the organization, and I want to honor the commitment I've made to my wife" acknowledges their feelings while asserting your needs. Turning people down with Words to Lose—"I'm sorry, *but* there's *no way* I can take this on. You *have to* understand how overloaded I've been these last few years"—would only cause estrangement.

KINDNESS DOES NOT MEAN CONSTANT COMPLIANCE

"Being humble doesn't mean one has to be a mat."
—MAYA ANGELOU

Being kind doesn't mean always going along to get along. Ann and her next-door neighbor were stay-at-home moms. They shared play groups, car pooling, and chauffeuring for five years. Then Ann's friend Jackie was hired by a bakery to work from nine to two, which was perfect because it meant Jackie would be home by the time her three kids returned from school.

At least that was the way it worked in theory. The first week on the job, Jackie called Ann to explain that the owner of the bakery had asked her to work late. Would Ann please watch her children until she got home? Ann was glad to help.

Another emergency delayed Jackie the subsequent week, and the next, and before Ann knew it, she was tending Jackie's brood almost every afternoon. She resented her neighbor for taking advantage of her generosity and for assuming she would always be available for free.

Ann discussed her dilemma with me. She didn't want to play nanny any more, but she didn't want to lose her long-time friend. I suggested she visualize the scale of needs to see how out of balance they were. She had been bending over backward to meet Jackie's needs while hers and those of her children were being disregarded. It wasn't insensitive of her to speak up about the situation, it was smart.

Ann decided to stand up for herself and solve Jackie's situation at the same time. She asked a teenager in the neighborhood if she might be interested in watching Jackie's children. The high schooler was delighted at the prospect of earning some spending money. Ann then sat down with Jackie and explained that while she had been happy to help her, starting the first of the month, she wanted to have her afternoons open so she could run errands and spend time with her own children. Ann gave Jackie the name of the baby-sitter, mentioning that the young woman had already expressed interest and was willing to work cheap because she already knew and liked Jackie's kids . . . and the two-block commute.

I CAN'T SAY NO

"Every time you say 'no' to a request for time, money, energy, or support, you are saying 'yes' to something else." —MAGGIE BEDROSIAN

At this point, someone in the audience always asks, "What if I reject a request and the person gets mad at me?" In her delightful book *Life Is More Than Your To-Do List*, author Maggie Bedrosian suggests you can become more comfortable "giving regrets" if you understand that behind every no is a yes; that when you turn *away* from one thing, you turn *toward* something else. Some people frantically try to be everything to everyone and end up being nothing to the people they care most about. What's really important to you? Your time and energy are limited resources. Don't squander them on trivialities. Identify your resounding raison d'être so you can say "Sorry" to activities that would rob you of precious time with your real priorities.

One woman thanked me for teaching her this technique because it had helped her be more assertive with her demanding mother. Rhoda laughed and said, "You've heard the saying 'My mother is a travel agent for guilt trips?' That's my mom. She calls every day asking for something. She used to run me ragged because I was afraid to say no to her. Last week she called and asked me to drive her to the mall. I didn't have time that afternoon, and offered to take her on Saturday when we go together with my daughters. That wasn't good enough for her, and she started in on her poor-me routine."

"Visualizing the scale helped me see how much I've catered to my mother's needs over the years. I love my mom, but in this situation it was fair for me to say I couldn't do it. I explained my other commitments, and offered to go with her on the weekend or to call a senior citizens van if it was important she go that day. She harrumphed a little, but I didn't feel guilty because the scale helped me see that I was justified in turning her down."

KNOW WHAT YOU STAND FOR

"If you don't stand for something, you'll fall for anything."

—ANONYMOUS

What do you stand for? The first-century Jewish teacher Hillel the Elder asked, "If I am not for myself, who will be for me? If I am for myself alone, what am I? And if not now, when?" Those timeless words eloquently express the importance of serving ourselves while serving others. If you don't learn how and when to say no, you'll pay the steep price of self-sacrifice.

As Amy Tan, author of the best-seller *The Joy Luck Club,* observed, "I did not lose myself all at once. I rubbed out my face over the years." Stand for a fair balance in the needs being met and you won't take a fall when pushed to say yes.

ACTION PLAN FOR SAYING NO

Your company prides itself on being one of the biggest contributors to a local charity. They are targeting 100 percent involvement this year, and your division leader is pressuring everyone in your office to commit to a large donation. You respect their efforts, however you already give a substantial portion of your salary to another nonprofit organization. How do you respond when the leader asks you for money?

WORDS TO LOSE

You find yourself coerced by the pleas of the campaign leader.
"How can I say no? I'll be the only one in the office who doesn't give anything."

Your fear of being ostracized rules your thinking. You're reluctant to break ranks.
"What will my coworkers say? They'll think I'm cheap."

The campaign chair doesn't want to take no for an answer.
"He's making me feel like I'm a bad person for not donating. Maybe I should just give in and get it over with."

WORDS TO USE

You envision the scale of needs to see if it's in balance.
"I understand the charity deserves to be supported, and I deserve the right to decide the group I want to donate to."

You conclude that it's fair for you to respectfully say no.
"I hope your campaign is successful, and I have already committed to supporting another charity."

You remind yourself that you are not being selfish, and think of your resounding raison d'être so you don't cave in to pressure.
"I agree it's important to support our local charities, and that's why I already donate to the one of my choice."

> "THE MISFORTUNE IN CONVERSATION IS THIS:
> PEOPLE GO ON WITHOUT KNOWING HOW
> TO GET OFF."
> —SAMUEL JOHNSON

· Chapter 23 ·

Terminate Tactfully

Would you like to know what to do if someone won't stop talking?

This dilemma is brought up in almost every Tongue Fu! workshop. Everyone wants to learn, "How can you exit a conversation without appearing rude?" Popular UPI advice columnist Abigail Van Buren featured this common complaint in a 1995 column. A reader complained that a needy friend called her a minimum of four times a week and rattled on for at least an hour each time. The reader said she made her living talking to the public eight hours a day and the last thing she wanted to do when she got home was talk on the phone. Despite hints or an outright "I've got to go," her friend continued to carry on. The reader didn't want to hurt her friend's feelings but it had gotten to the point where she hated to answer her own phone.

Abby suggested the woman say, "I'm sorry, I can't talk to you now. I'll call you later," and then hang up. She noted that later could be tomorrow, next week, or next month. She also suggested the reader get an answering machine so she could screen her calls and that she should commit this homily to memory: "Nobody can walk all over me unless I lie down first."

Dear Abby's advice is certainly one way to handle this prevalent problem. The word "problem" is used intentionally because there is definitely something wrong with people who carry on soliloquies, never asking or caring if the other person is interested in what they have to say.

STOP NONSTOP TALKERS

"The man who lets himself be bored is even more contemptible than the bore."
—SAMUEL BUTLER

There are a variety of ways to deflate windbags. These techniques can help you *tactfully terminate* interminable monologues so you are no longer at the mercy of people who like to hear themselves talk.

1. *Check the needs being met.* In the case of Dear Abby's reader, the needs were clearly out of balance and had been for a long time. It's time for her to stop taking it.

2. Don't suffer in silence while you wait for her to stop talking. It may never happen. *Interrupt her, being sure to say her name.* Yes, I said interrupt. Saying her name will cause him to pause for just a second, and that is your chance to get your verbal foot in the door. I know you've been taught it's rude to interrupt, and normally that's true. However, who is being rude in this situation? You are not insensitive to gracefully bring a one-sided conversation to a close; the person who has the audacity to carry on about herself ad infinitum is the one being thoughtless.

3. *Summarize what she has been saying.* Paraphrasing what one has said convinces her you've been listening and is the key to an inoffensive exit. Reflecting

what she has said gives the conversation a sense of closure.

4. *Put the conversation in the past with a wrap-up statement.* An excellent way to end overlong business interactions is to say, "As soon as I hang up, I'm going to . . ." or "Right after we finish talking, I'll be sure to . . ." For personal conversations, close with a polite Word to Use: "I wish I had more time to talk with you, and I need to get dinner started." or "I wish I could hear about your son's piano recital, and I've got to get back to . . ."

5. *Close with finality and a friendly phrase.* Pleasant phrases such as "I *appreciate* you bringing this to my attention" or "I'll *look forward* to following up on that suggestion" or "I'm *glad* to know you're doing well" offset any brusqueness in your tone. Make sure your voice ends with warm yet firm downward inflection. If you trail off tentatively or end with an "Okay?" you'll throw the conversational ball right back in the other person's lap.

PHONE—FRIEND OR FOE?

"The secret of making one's self tiresome is not to know when to stop."
—ANONYMOUS

Right at this point in one of my seminars, a college counselor volunteered this positive response: "That idea is worth a thousand dollars to me." I smiled and asked why.

"Many of my students are living away from home for the first time, and they're lonely and confused. As a gesture of support, I've given many of them my home phone number. Well, you know the rest of the story. I spend anywhere from two to three hours a night on the phone with them. I can't bring myself to hang up on them.

That seems so heartless. The trouble is, I'm burned out because I never have any time to recharge my batteries. Plus my husband is really beginning to resent the fact that I'm on the phone half the night.

"I've been serving my students' needs, but I haven't done a very good job of serving ours. From now on, students are welcome to phone me at home if it's an emergency. If they call, I'll be glad to spend ten or fifteen minutes with them and then use Tactful Termination: "I'm sorry to hear you don't like your professor. As soon as we hang up, I'll make a note to check out some other instructors in that department. I've got an appointment open tomorrow morning. Why don't you come by then and we'll see what we can do about lining you up with a different teacher? I'll look forward to seeing you in the morning."

COURTEOUSLY CLOSE OVERLONG CONVERSATIONS

"Half the world is composed of people who have something to say and can't, and the other half who have nothing to say and keep saying it."
—ROBERT FROST

A woman in that same session said, "This idea works in business, but how about social situations? I went to a singles dance last weekend and was backed into a corner by this incredibly narcissistic guy. You've heard the line about the egotist who says, 'Well, enough about me. What do *you* think about me?' That was him. This boor's idea of conversation was waiting for my mouth to stop moving so he could talk some more about himself. There was no escaping him."

If you have the misfortune to be collared by someone from the half who have nothing to say and keep saying it, remember the balance of needs. If someone is insensitive enough to monopolize your time, it is wise, not rude, to bring the inequitable conversation to a close. This woman could have said, "Craig, thanks for your tips about the Internet. You're right, it sounds like something I might want to look into. I'm going to go try some of those refreshments. Thanks for talking with me," and then walk away with a warm smile and a firm step.

Are you thinking this technique is a blazing attack of the obvious? Well, as the title of Robert Fulghum's best-selling book states, *Maybe, Maybe Not.* I shared this story during one presentation and a woman laughed out loud. "I could have used this idea last night. A salesman called right in the middle of dinner and kept me on the phone forever! I kept waiting for him to shut up, but he never took a breath! I missed my favorite TV show."

The rest of the group confessed they'd had similar experiences. I asked them, "Who decides whether to answer the phone? Who controls how long we stay on the phone? Who determines whether we miss our favorite TV show?" If you're sure you don't want to buy the telemarketer's product or service, don't wait until he finishes his spiel. End the intrusion with a polite "Thank you, I'm not interested," and gently replace the phone on the hook. You're saving the salesperson time that won't result in a deal, and you're giving yourself more time with those people or things you value more highly.

DIPLOMATICALLY DEFLECT

"Are you riding the horse, or is the horse riding you?"
—TONGUE FU'ISM

You may want to know how to keep someone from starting to talk in the first place. In another of my workshops, a receptionist named Lenora put the question this way: "Some employees and visitors expect me to drop whatever I'm doing whenever they want to chat. I don't want to be unsociable, but I can't sit there and listen to them yak. I've got work to do. How can I let people know I don't have time to talk without seeming unfriendly?"

The key to being suitably sociable is to ride the horse, instead of letting it ride you. In my book *Concentration: How to Focus for Success,* I maintain that the key to being graciously effective in an office environment is to "have the courage to diplomatically impose on time, people, and events your decision as to what's important and what must come first." This Diplomatic Deflection technique can help you tactfully take charge of your work setting.

1. Whenever someone interrupts to ask or tell you something, immediately find out his or her purpose. Then ask yourself, "Is this *more* important than what I was doing?" If it is, by all means, switch your attention.

2. If it's not, have the courage to reschedule the intrusion. Yes, it's important to be accessible, but at what cost? If you consistently honor other people's wishes before your own, your performance will suffer the consequences. *You* must determine who and what you focus on, when and for how long. Be sure to use positive phrasing to change what might otherwise be a discourteous dismissal into a diplomatic deflection.

   - *Start off with the person's name* (it ensures you have his attention) and *express your intention to deal with the situation.* Acknowledge the importance of the situation by saying "I want to discuss this with you" or "I realize you need an answer to this" instead of turning the person away with a *"I can't* talk to you now" or brushing them off with "This will have to wait."
   - *Continue by explaining your previous commitment* or must-be-completed-first priority *prefaced by the word "and."* Say *"and* I promised Mrs. Moore I'd call back with . . ." or ". . . *and* I need to finish this agenda for the nine A.M. staff briefing."
   - Next *ask, "Could you come back this afternoon?"* or "Can I call you right after I . . . ?" Requesting cooperation produces a lot more receptivity than ordering someone around with a "You'll have to come back when it's not so crazy" or com-

plaining about how busy you are with "I'm way behind . . . I don't have time for that now." Finally, *close
graciously* by saying, "Thanks for understanding. I
appreciate you agreeing to . . ."

Previous participants who have made it a habit to use Tactful
Termination and Diplomatic Deflection say it's made a measur-
able difference in their productivity. One supervisor confessed, "I
used to come in early and stay late because I couldn't get any work
done during the day. Now I ask myself if what the other person
wants is the *best* use of my time and attention. I was initially worried I might offend people by putting them off, but just the opposite has happened. Several associates have mentioned they
admire my determination to stick to my priorities, and they've
asked if I could teach them how to do the same."

ACTION PLAN FOR TACTFUL TERMINATION

You're at the mall and you run into someone you used to work with. You're happy to see her, but you're short on time. She greets you with a big hug and excitedly starts telling you about her engagement. What do you do?

WORDS TO LOSE	WORDS TO USE
You inwardly groan and resign yourself to not having time to find the items you wanted. *"Hello, Jennifer, it's been a long time, hasn't it? Tell me how you've been doing."*	You think of the scale of needs and determine to keep them balanced. *"Jennifer, you look great. Do you have time for a walk/talk next week? I'd love to have a chance to catch up with you."*
You agree to a cup of coffee even though you rather not. *"Uh, yeah, a cup of coffee would be nice. Is there a place here in the mall?"*	You diplomatically decline the cup of coffee because you're clear about your priorities. *"I wish I had time for some coffee, and I have only an hour left to get a present for my son."*
You look at your watch regretfully and realize you're going to have to make another trip back. *"I guess I'm just going to have to come to the mall another time."*	You tactfully terminate the conversation while being sensitive to her feelings and while honoring your own needs. *"I'm so glad we're back in touch. I'll look forward to . . ."*

· Chapter 24 ·
Act and Feel Confident

Would you like to know how to project confidence so you command people's respect?

Many rehabilitated criminals explain their modus operandi was to prey on people who looked as if they could easily be intimidated, people with weak posture (stooped shoulders, eyes cast downward, tentative steps) who looked like they'd be an easy mark. In contrast, kung fu masters carry themselves with an assurance that actually prevents physical attacks. Tongue Fu! masters want to do the verbal equivalent—to conduct themselves with a quiet confidence that deters others from all kinds of abuse.

COWER OR TOWER?

"If a man harbors any sort of fear, it percolates through all his thinking, damages his personality, makes him landlord to a ghost."
—HENRY WARD BEECHER

You can discover for yourself the dramatic difference between feeling fearful and feeling forceful with this simple five-second exercise. It's especially effective if you ask someone else to help you so you can see with your own eyes the difference between a "poor me" and a "proud me" posture.

Please stand up. Now let your shoulders fall forward and sag. Let your chest sink in, drop your head, and look down at the floor. Put your feet close together and assume the "fig leaf" position (hands clasped in front of you). Don't you feel hesitant and unsure of yourself?

Now pull your shoulders up and back, (which automatically pulls your head up, straightens your posture, and brings your hands to your sides). Place your feet squarely on the ground, hip width apart. Don't you feel more confident and sure of yourself?

THE FIVE-SECOND CONFIDENCE FIX

"Man is made by his beliefs. As he believes, so he is."
—BHAGAVAD GITA

The Five-Second Confidence Fix is an easy way to act confident so you feel confident. If you're depressed, you probably have droopy posture. Your spine and your spirits are sagging. Dismiss the doldrums and free yourself from fear by squaring your shoulders, lifting your chin, and assuming a more athletic stance, your weight balanced on your feet. You'll instantly feel more optimistic because things are, literally and figuratively, looking up. Hold your head up high and you'll be less vulnerable to mental marauders seeking victims.

I can happily report that the Five-Second Confidence Fix works wonders in the real world. Our two sons, Andrew and Tom, auditioned for the Maui production of *Peter Pan.* With visions of Lost Boys dancing in their heads, they eagerly filled out the necessary forms and waited for their turns to try out.

After twenty obviously seasoned young professionals auditioned, Tom walked onstage in front of the sizable theater audience, sang one stanza of his song, and promptly forgot the rest. He struggled through the rest of the song, then had to make the agonizingly long walk back to his seat, where he sank down, fighting back tears.

The longer he thought about the experience, the lower he slumped into the seat. I could tell he was about to cry, so I said, "Sit proud, Tom." He pulled himself up and his whole demeanor changed. He went from crushed to confident.

If Tom hadn't altered his physical position, he would have continued to dwell on what he saw as his humiliation. He would have avoided any further tryouts in the future. Instead, later that evening, he and his brother were happily discussing their hopes for a callback.

Remember this the next time you try something and it doesn't work out. If you are down in the dumps, change the way you hold your body to change the way you feel. Use the Five-Second Confidence Fix and you can go from feeling glum and heavyhearted to feeling glad and lighthearted.

IT'S ALL IN YOUR HEAD

"Doubt is a pain too lonely to know that faith is his brother."
—KAHLIL GIBRAN

Do you have an event coming up that's making your knees knock and your palms sweat? Are you planning to attend your spouse's office Christmas party? Are you in the finals of a chess tournament, playing an individual rated higher than you are? Do you need to counsel an employee who's got an "It's not in my job description" attitude?

Would you like to walk into that situation with poise rather than panic? You can if you use visualization to turn your self-doubt into decisiveness. Visualization is the single best thing you can do to improve your performance in any area. That's a bold statement, isn't it? These four behavioral insights explain how and why visualization works:

1. *Confidence is based on recent, frequent, successful practice.*

Wouldn't you agree that if you do something well and have done it often and recently, you can walk into that situation with confidence? That's what confidence is . . . feeling "I can" due to proven competence.

2. *Nervousness is caused by focusing on your doubts and fears.*
   If you're thinking, "How did I get myself into this? What if I choke in front of all those people?" you'll be apprehensive. Nervousness is a manifestation of dwelling on misgivings.

3. *People are uncomfortable in unfamiliar situations.*
   The fight-or-flight response is an instinctive survival mechanism. When you are in an unfamiliar environment, your body pumps adrenaline though your system so you have the energy necessary to defend yourself or escape. When you don't know your surroundings well, you're in a state of anxiety (defined in two words as "not knowing"). Only after you've spent time in a place and know it's safe, can you relax and release the tension that accompanies new circumstances.

4. *Mental practice is perfect practice that makes you better, faster than actual practice.*
   Real-life practice is certainly beneficial, but it's impossible to perform the activity perfectly every time, so you imprint mistakes and subpar performance. The perfect practice that is possible through mental imaging accelerates improvement and skill acquisition because you can do it right every time.

WORRY VS. REHEARSE

"Fear makes strangers of people who could be friends."

—SHIRLEY MacLAINE

I introduced this idea of visualization in a seminar I gave, and a woman named Martha voiced her doubts. "My son is getting married next month. Every time I picture his big day, I break into hives. Thinking about it makes me feel worse, not better. I'm starting to dread his wedding."

I was curious as to what Martha was picturing when she thought about the wedding, so I asked, "Don't you like the bride?"

"No, that's not it," she corrected. "My son's fiancée is lovely. It's just that she is the only daughter in a very prominent family here in town, and they're throwing a lavish reception. Her parents are wealthy jet-setters, and we don't have anything in common. I sat next to them at the engagement dinner and couldn't think of a thing to say the entire evening. I just know I'm going to feel out of place at this fancy shindig, surrounded by three hundred of their best friends."

When asked how much time was left before the ceremony, she answered, "Three weeks." I said, "Martha, you can spend the next three weeks *worrying,* or you can spend the next three weeks *rehearsing.* You can talk yourself into apprehension, or you can talk yourself into anticipation. What's it going to be?"

I suggested she use the following guidelines to make her visualization a *positive* preparation. I explained that visualization can work for or against you, depending on your focus. By picturing the right things over and over, she could accumulate confidence and turn her dread into determination.

1. *Duplicate the real-life situation as closely as possible.* What will the church look like? Where will you be seated? Fill in as many details as you can and involve all your senses. You want to put yourself there in your mind. Mental practice is less useful if you jump around from scene to scene. You can set up a feeling of flow by visualizing sequentially from beginning to end. That way you're familiarizing yourself with what will happen that day, so you'll have already "been there, done that."

2. *Picture what you don't want to happen, and plan how you're going to respond.*

You may be thinking, "Isn't this contradictory? If I focus on my fears, won't it make me more nervous?" It does if you just dwell on *all* the awful things that could happen. Take it one step further, though, and plan how you can handle your worst-nightmare scenario with poise. Anticipate what could go wrong and figure out how you're going to keep your cool no matter what. Instead of imagining yourself intimidated by all the strangers, picture yourself as a gracious hostess, seeking out new friends and making sure family members feel welcome. Instead of avoiding the bride's parents, picture yourself approaching them, shaking their hands, and complimenting them on the time and effort they poured into making this day special.

3. *Positively phrase and practice exactly how you want to perform over and over.*

Be sure to express your desired performance in *positive* rather than negative terms. Instead of saying, "I'm going to feel self-conscious," tell yourself, "I am going to extend myself to the people who cared enough to honor my son with their presence on this special day." Instead of thinking, "I'm so threatened by these famous celebrities," think, "I'm glad I'm here and I'm going to enjoy every minute of the ceremony."

Martha wrote me after the wedding, saying, "That day was everything I could have hoped for. I didn't realize I was talking myself into a state of dread with all those doom-and-gloom predictions. Someone once told me that 'worrying is just a way of praying for what you *don't* want.' I think visualization is a way of praying for, and producing, what you *do* want."

SPEAK YOUR MIND CONFIDENTLY

"Mend your speech a little, lest you mar your fortunes."
—WILLIAM SHAKESPEARE

It's presumptuous to think I could improve on Shakespeare, however wouldn't you agree you should mend your speech a little so you can *make* your fortunes? Power is the ability to get things done. Your power depends on your ability to educate and motivate through words. If you want to be effective, it's important to master the art and skill of expressing yourself confidently.

Yet in a survey cited in *The Book of Lists,* more people feared public speaking than death. When a participant in one of my workshops asked how this could be, a fellow attendee quipped, "That's obvious. We only have to die once." People of all ages and at all levels of experience admit to being paralyzed at the thought of speaking before a group.

You can overcome this fear and learn how to speak your mind by using the three guidelines to visualization listed in the last section and by seeking to *inform* rather than *impress.* If you're feeling self-conscious, it's because you're focusing on yourself ("How do I look? What do they think of me?"). If you switch your focus to your audience ("What could make this time well spent for them? "How can they benefit from these ideas?"), you'll no longer be obsessed with doubts. Your anxiety will be overridden by a sense of mission to provide value.

TURN PANIC INTO POISE

"Argue for your limitations, and sure enough, they're yours."
—RICHARD BACH, AUTHOR OF
JONATHAN LIVINGSTON SEAGULL

One man's success story illustrates how mental rehearsal can turn fright into delight. Kevin had been asked to present a paper at his professional association's national convention. He confessed he was scared to death. "I've never spoken to a group of more than fifty people in my whole life, and there's supposed to be over five hundred people in my session. I'm afraid I'll get up there and make a fool of myself in front of my peers."

I said, "Kevin, you can argue for your limitations or you can eliminate them. Commit to doing this five-minute visualization exercise for the next ten nights. Pick a time at the end of the day so you're not distracted by other obligations. Sit quietly and picture the room where your session will be held. If you haven't been there before, it's worth a call to the hotel to ask for a description.

"Imagine being introduced and bounding up to the platform with energetic, purposeful strides. See yourself looking out at the audience, smiling, and making friendly eye contact with at least one individual in each quarter of the room. Imagine feeling grateful for this opportunity to share your ideas and insights.

"Picture yourself PAUSING until you have everyone's attention. See yourself making your points in an organized, understandable way and projecting clearly to the back of the room. Visualize yourself reaching out to the audience and caring that they get something of value from your presentation. Imagine yourself closing with a call to action that inspires everyone to carry out your ideas."

Kevin called me the day after the convention. "It worked! I was so comfortable up there, it felt like I'd done it a hundred times before!" He *had* done it a hundred times before—in his mind.

Does visualization guarantee success? No, it guarantees an improved performance. John F. Kennedy said, "Not everything that is faced can be changed . . . but nothing can be changed that is not faced." Your real-life events may not go as you "scripted" them in your visualization; however, they will certainly go more smoothly and successfully than if you walked in cold. Face down your fears with visualization and you can transform potentially traumatic events into triumphs.

ACTION PLAN FOR ACTING AND FEELING CONFIDENT

Your twenty-fifth high school reunion is a week away. You're eager to see your long-lost buddies, but you've gained quite a bit of weight over the years. You're considering passing up this event rather than enduring everyone's shocked looks. How do you spend your thought time?

WORDS TO LOSE	WORDS TO USE
You talk yourself into a state of dread and apprehension. *"I'm going to be so embarrassed when everyone sees how heavy I've gotten."*	You talk yourself into a state of determination and anticipation. *"I'm looking forward to getting together with my friends and catching up."*
You focus on your doubts and fears and increase your nervousness. *"Everyone else is probably going to look great. I'm going to feel so conspicuous and self-conscious."*	You use visualization to mentally rehearse how you want the evening to go. *"I am going to have fun finding out what's happened to Joyce and Kelly. And I'm going to dance every dance."*
You worry about what could go wrong. You obsess about the event until you decide not to go. *"Forget it. I'm not going to put myself through that. It would be humiliating, and I just wouldn't be able to relax and enjoy myself."*	You familiarize yourself with the location, and picture yourself walking in and towering instead of cowering. *"I am going to stand tall and make the most of this marvelous opportunity to reunite with my high school chums."*

· Chapter 25 ·

Five Principles of Persuasion

Are you ready to speak up for what you want? Merely having a valid case isn't enough. You must first summon the courage to speak up for yourself, and then present your ideas with timing, sensitivity, and skill so your listener is motivated to say yes.

As American essayist Joseph Wood Krutch observed, "Cats seem to go on the principle that it doesn't do any harm to ask for what you want." If it works for cats, maybe it can work for you.

Shelley, an athletic friend of mine who works as a law clerk in a Washington, D.C., law firm, spent every noon hour jogging on the paths bordering the Smithsonian. She loved getting outside for the exercise, but she didn't enjoy having to change back into her professional clothes without the benefit of a shower. She approached the partners and proposed that a woman's locker room be installed, similar to the one provided for male employees. They turned her down flat, citing the expense, lack of space, and so on. Shelley called me and asked for help.

The first thing I did was compliment her on not relinquishing her dream. I suggested she could forge her own fate and make her dream come true if she presented her proposal using these Five Principles of Persuasion.

FORTUNE VS. FATE

"We make our fortunes and call them fate." —BENJAMIN DISRAELI

1. *Approach the situation with positive expectations.*
   You may think this suggestion rather obvious. As someone in one of my groups pointed out, "That's common sense. We know that." In reply, I quoted something my dad used to say: "Just because something is common sense doesn't mean it's common practice."

   Have you ever approached someone with a proposal while inside you were thinking, "This is a waste of time. They'll never approve this." If *you* don't believe your suggestion stands a chance, how can they? Dwight D. Eisenhower once observed, "Pessimism never won any battle." Talk yourself into a state of optimism ("I know this is worthwhile") so you can go in with the courage of your convictions.

2. *Anticipate and voice their objections.*
   Figure out why they might say no. Determine why they might turn you down, and then state their arguments first. If you don't preface your points with their objections, they won't even be listening to you; they'll be waiting for their turn to talk so they can tell you why your recommendation won't work. If you predict they'll protest with "We don't have the money for this in our budget," then guess what the first words out of your mouth better be? "You may be thinking we don't have the funds available, *and* if I can have your attention for the next ten minutes, I can show how we'll save this amount of money in the first three weeks of operation."

3. *Number and document each point.*
   My high school debate coach used to tell his de-

baters: "Your expertise is judged by the organization of your thoughts." You may be the world's foremost authority on the matter you're presenting, but if your argument is disorganized, listeners will conclude you don't know what you're talking about.

The easiest and quickest way to lend legitimacy to points is to number them. "There are three reasons why this addition will be worthwhile. The first is . . . , the second is . . . ," and so forth. Enumerating evidence makes material sound like facts rather than opinion so it carries more weight. Furthermore, listeners can understand and remember what's being said more easily because of the clear structure.

As a member of the National Speakers Association and a professional speaker for over fifteen years, I've learned the most powerful way to get a message across is to follow this pattern: make a point, give an example; make a point, give an example. Examples serve double duty. Audiences remember examples, which remind them of your points, and examples also provide proof of the benefits of what you're proposing.

4. *Meet their needs and speak their language.*
Avoid using the word *I,* as in "I think a locker room will be good for our employees." People won't do things for *your* reasons; they'll do them for their own. Paul Harlan Collins offers a couple of *Today's Chuckle* one-liners that illustrate how parents can master this principle: "The best way to get your teenager to shovel the driveway . . . is to tell him he can use the car," and "If you want to teach your kids to count . . . give them different allowances."

Ask yourself what's most important to the person you're trying to persuade. Money, safety, reputation, status, power? Figure out how your proposal will benefit him and then address those advantages. If what's important to him is his reputation as a leader in this field, then emphasize how he will be the first to implement this innovative idea and that his pioneering efforts will set the standard for years to come.

5. *Motivate them to "try on" your ideas.*
   Ralph Waldo Emerson realized, "To know how to suggest is the great art of teaching." The same is true of persuasion. If you pressure people to see the wisdom of your arguments, they may turn you down simply because they don't like reasoning being forced down their throats. The goal is to actively involve them with questions and stories so they *see* what you're *saying*. As soon as they picture what is being proposed, they're out of the passive, resistive mode and imagining your idea as if it were a done deal.

REVERSE REFUSALS WITH THE THREE R'S

"Never change a winning game, always change a losing one."
—VINCE LOMBARDI, SR.

My friend Shelley said, "If I had presented my original proposal using these five principles, I probably would have won. Now I'm afraid it's too late and I've lost out. The partners aren't going to give me another chance now that they've refused me."

She had a good point. Once people have said no, the case is often closed. However, you can reopen a dead issue *if* you unearth and introduce new evidence. Bring a new point to their attention, one not discussed in the initial negotiation. They now have justification for changing their minds and reaching a different conclusion. They can reverse themselves without losing face because you have given them new criteria on which to base a decision. As respected football coach Vince Lombardi suggested, if your original tactics weren't victorious, it's time to try different ones.

I recommended that Shelley motivate the partners to reconsider her request by using the Three Rs. If you have recently been turned down concerning something you want, take heart, and heed this advice.

Retreat: Exit the situation gracefully. Don't slam the door on your way out because you may want to walk back through it. Accept the no gracefully so the door will be open when you want to try again.

Reevaluate: Why did they say no? Did you not address their needs? Did you forget to number your points so your evidence was underwhelming? Improve areas in which you were weak and uncover proof not used the first time.

Reapproach: Schedule a new appointment and preface your remarks with "I know we've talked about this before, and I've uncovered some information that casts new light on the situation." Then present your ideas incorporating the Five Rules of Persuasion and Words to Use.

Shelley succeeded in getting the lockers approved the second time around because she did her homework. She contacted a national fitness association and obtained data regarding the financial advantages of employees who exercise during their lunch hour. She located other corporations who were glad to talk about the workmen's compensation benefits they'd reaped from installing changing/shower facilities. Shelley neutralized the partners' objections about lack of space by demonstrating the advantages of converting a little-used conference room. Later she called to give me the good news and added a variation of Yogi Berra's often-quoted line "Looks like it's not over 'til the *fit* lady sings."

PERSUADE, DON'T PRESSURE

*"In teaching it is the method and not the content that is the message . . .
the drawing out, not the pumping in."* —ASHLEY MONTAGU

A participant in one of my sessions said, "I understand all of this
except the Fifth Principle. How exactly do you get someone to 'try
on' your ideas?"

He had brought up a good point. How *can* you get people to
reconsider and embrace your ideas? Take a tip from Socrates, who
wisely understood that people remember more of what they learn
themselves than what is force fed.

The Socratic method of turning statements into rhetorical questions is pivotal to successful persuasion. It's the difference between
pressuring someone to make up his mind and presenting the ideas
in a provocative fashion that allows him to make up his own mind.
You can reverse resistance by actively engaging people and putting
them in the mental driver's seat. For example, rather than stating,
"I think our female employees deserve a place to change after they
work out," ask, "Would you like to see how we could reduce our
sick leave and workmen's compensation costs by installing locker
rooms for our female employees?"

TELL ME A STORY

*"Anecdotes are sometimes the best vehicles of truth, and if striking and
appropriate are often more impressive and powerful than argument."*
—TYRONE EDWARDS

Questions and success stories with sensory details move listeners
from their logical left brain to their emotional right brain. Even
the toughest critics enjoy hearing an interesting, well-told tale.
Once listeners are interested in the outcome of your anecdote,
they're experiencing your idea. Vivid word pictures have the power
to transform rhetoric into personal reality.

An associate of mine proudly passed her real estate exam and obtained her license. After countless open houses, Maria still hadn't made one sale. She trudged into her supervisor's office, collapsed into the chair by his desk, and exclaimed, "I quit!"

He said, "How can you quit? You've only been an agent for a few months." She disconsolately explained, "I've logged over four thousand miles on my car, worked with dozens of clients, and I don't have anything to show for it. I've come to the conclusion that old adage 'You can lead a horse to water, but you can't make him drink' is correct."

Her wise boss countered, "Maria, you're not supposed to make them drink. You're supposed to make them *thirsty.*"

Over lunch, Maria and I discussed how she could use the Five Principles of Persuasion and the Three Rs (retreat, reevaluate, reapproach) in her real estate career. Questions and stories now make up a large part of her marketing. She'll say, "Isn't this a lovely neighborhood?" instead of "I like this part of town," and "Who would be in this room, Tina or Dolores?" instead of "I think this is a pretty room." She asks the current or previous residents what their favorite memories of the house are so she can personalize it for her clients. Needless to say, she's met with considerably more success because she is making her buyers thirsty rather than pressuring them to drink.

ACTION PLAN FOR FIVE PRINCIPLES OF PERSUASION

Your kids are having an end-of-the-summer pool party, and the energetic youngsters are running wild. You have told them several times to stop roughhousing, but they continue with their antics. How do you persuade them to calm down?

WORDS TO LOSE	WORDS TO USE
You yell at them and warn them you're at the end of your patience. *"Unless you kids stop horsing around, I'm going to throw you out and the party's over."*	You put some thought into what you're going to say so you'll be more persuasive. *"How can I get them to see how this benefits them?"*
You tell yourself it's a waste of time. *"They're not going to obey me. They're so wound up, they wouldn't listen to Attila the Hun."*	You convince yourself this is significant and doable. *"Kids, please come sit down at the table and give me your eyes. I have something important to discuss."*
You take charge and tell them what you want and why you want them to calm down. *"You guys are going to get hurt. I went to all this effort to put on a nice party, and you're ruining it."*	You tell them a story that illustrates why it's in their best interests to quiet down. *"Do you know what happened to Kevin last year? Kevin was running and he slipped . . ."*
You wrap up your lecture about how important safety is. *"Now, I better not have to tell you this again. Do you hear?"*	You ask them what their understanding is of the agreement. *"So, what are the pool rules if you want to swim here?"*

· Chapter 26 ·

Break Free from Bullies

What if you try all these techniques and they don't work? You're probably dealing with a bully, someone who knowingly and purposely rolls over people.

Avoiding bullies who willfully abuse people is the best policy. Proverbs 15:18 in the Bible advises, "Keep away from angry, short-tempered men, lest you learn to be like them and endanger your soul." Realistically, that's not always possible. If you work, live, or deal with someone who deliberately uses aggression to manipulate or control others, this chapter is for you.

INNOCENT OR INTENTIONAL?

"All cruelty springs from hard-heartedness and weakness." —SENECA

The Tongue Fu! techniques covered up to this point work with most people. I believe 90 percent of difficult behavior is situational, a by-product of an event that has made the person unhappy. If you interact with these people sensitively and skillfully, you can often resolve the situation amicably. The other 10 percent of difficult behavior is intentional rather than innocent. Such people require special handling because they often act illogically and don't respond to reason.

How can you tell if a stranger is a habitual brute or just upset? You will probably be able to sense it. Some people don't seem very pleasant, but you can tell they are caught up in the emotions associated with something that actually happened and you unfortunately just happen to be the lightening rod for their thunder. With these people, you will feel some human response. They can perhaps be placated.

Bullies, on the other hand, badger you to achieve their end. You may feel a calculated malevolence exuding from them, and at a gut level, you perceive that they're deliberately undermining you in an attempt to feel superior. They may actually delight in your squirming and increase their efforts to make you suffer.

IS THEIR BEHAVIOR DELIBERATE AND/OR DANGEROUS?

"It is difficult to be convinced of one's superiority unless one can make the inferior suffer in some obvious way." —MAX RADIN

We'll talk about how to handle bullies in the next few pages. First we need to discuss how to handle the small segment of this difficult 10 percent who are pathological. These individuals run rampant over those in their way, with no regard to consequences. These people were perhaps so abused or neglected as children that they simply don't care one way or the other about their fellow human beings. This group also includes substance abusers and people with mental disorders. Indications you might be dealing with a drug abuser are dilated pupils, a vacant stare or wild, rolling eyes, an unkempt appearance, extreme clumsiness, and slurred or nonsensical speech.

Don't mess with those in this dangerous faction. If you are standing in line for a Monster Truck rally and a thug crashes the line in front of you, ask yourself if it's worth hazarding your health to confront him. If you're walking down a snowy sidewalk and a gang of kids pelt you with slush balls, ask yourself if you could be jeopardizing your safety by telling them off. If someone wheels into the parking space you've been waiting for and then gives you the solitary salute, question whether you will be putting yourself in peril by pursuing them.

In today's violent world of armed physical assaults and attacks from strangers, adopting a pacifist attitude is not being a wimp, it's being wise. Better to sacrifice your pride than your life. By choosing your battles, you can put these events in perspective and realize that someone jumping in line or stealing your parking place does not warrant gambling away your well-being.

HOLD BULLIES ACCOUNTABLE FOR THEIR ACTIONS

"What we accept, we teach."   —ANONYMOUS

If you live with a chronic bully, I urge you to buy Patricia Evans's book *The Verbally Abusive Relationship: How to Recognize It and How to Respond.* As Evans points out,

> Verbal abuse is a means of holding power over another. It's a kind of battering which doesn't leave physical evidence, however it's just as painful. Because of the bully's need for dominance . . . he is compelled to negate the perceptions, experience, values, accomplishments, and plans of the other person, to constantly invalidate their reality. Verbal abuse can be vague, subtle, and unpredictable . . . yet it is insidious because the victim usually gets brainwashed, conditioned, and confused to the point they don't recognize the seriousness of their suffering.

Her book provides practical steps to setting limits and protecting your rights so you no longer accept or allow disparaging remarks of any kind.

YOU VS. I

"You might as well fall flat on your face as lean over too far backward."
—JAMES THURBER

Behavioral psychologists have found that most bullies behave as badly as they're allowed to. They don't hold themselves accountable for their actions—others must do it for them. How do you hold these pushy people responsible for their harmful behavior? Use the word *you.* Most assertiveness experts, rightfully so, emphasize the importance of using the word *I* when expressing your feelings. You're supposed to say, "I don't like it when you use that tone of voice," or "I'm disappointed that you forgot our date." In ordinary situations, it is appropriate to hold yourself accountable for your own emotions, not blame other people for how you feel.

Unfortunately, *I* statements don't work with bullies. If you say, "I don't like the way you're treating me," they'll retort, "That's your problem." Their attitude is "If you don't like this tone of voice . . . tough!" Or they'll launch a more aggressive attack designed to make you back off: "Stop making such a big deal about our date."

Instead, state your demands using the word *you* so *they* are answerable for their own actions. Say, "You need to speak to me with respect," or "From now on, you need to call if you're not going to show up for our date."

INTERNALIZE VS. INITIATE

"One of my problems is that I internalize everything. I can't express anger. I grow a tumor instead." —WOODY ALLEN

This concept of initiating rather than internalizing is one of the most important I've learned in my years of studying, speaking, and writing about this topic. Almost every time I present a seminar, someone will approach me at the break and tell me about how someone is mistreating them. My heart goes out to these caring, conscientious people because they are usually naively giving their best only to be kicked around or taken advantage of by some unscrupulous brute. They are hurt by the lack of justice in the situation and outraged that someone would treat them so badly. They often believe if they try hard enough, their loyalty, contributions, or goodness will be recognized and rewarded.

These psychologically abused individuals share a common trait. Most have internalized their angst rather than initiating action. When I ask if they've spoken to their persecutor about the situation, the answer is almost always no. They're afraid any assertiveness on their part would make the bully even more aggressive.

I counsel them to start using *you* words. It may sound wrong in the beginning, but it's the only way to get bullies to pay attention. Instead of examining themselves for fault, they need to put the responsibility where it belongs—on the bully. For example, they need to change what comes across as a whine, "I have so much to do, I'll never get caught up" (which elicits a heartless "You'll just have to stay late"), to "There are more projects than can get finished today. Which do you want as top priority, and which can wait until tommorrow?"

Instead of a weak "I don't feel it's fair for Barry to get that promotion," (which elicits a "Who said life is fair?"), say, "You promised me a promotion at the end of the quarter, and you need to honor that commitment." Rather than "I don't think it's right for you to take long lunch hours and expect me to cover for you," say, "You need to return to work on time so you're here for your one o'clock appointments."

HATING IS UNHEALTHY

"Like an unchecked cancer, hate corrodes the personality and eats away its vital unity." —MARTIN LUTHER KING, JR.

Hating an abuser serves no good purpose. As Lily Tomlin said, "The trouble with being in the rat race is that even if you win, you're still a rat." Take responsibility for your health, happiness, and peace of mind and don't let yourself get drawn into a race with a rat. Talk yourself through the Choose Your Battles criteria we covered earlier to determine whether it is prudent to confront your tormentor.

A friend of mine was assigned to an inspection team headed by an irascible individual. Les had respected the vast majority of his senior officers and found them to be models of integrity, but this mean-spirited man was infamous for tirades in which he would mercilessly berate his staff. Les was going to be working with this ogre for several weeks and knew he had to decide up front whether he was going to accept his verbal abuse. Was it worth throwing away a twenty-seven-year career in the military to "take him on" if it came to that? Les considered the consequences and made his decision.

The day of the briefing arrived. Les entered the officer's inner sanctum, introduced himself, put up his charts, and started his presentation. He hadn't completed his first point when the executive belligerently broke in and started raking him over the coals. Les stepped away from the easel, turned to the officer, and said firmly, "Sir, if you have questions about this briefing, if you have constructive comments about this inspection, I welcome them. YOU . . . WILL . . . NOT . . . CALL . . . ME . . . NAMES." Then he continued with his explanation of the agreed-upon procedures without further interruption.

Now, as famed radio broadcaster Paul Harvey would say, you may be wondering about" the rest of the story." Les, the man who gave the briefing, is my husband. A couple of months after this incident we attended a concert at an outdoor amphitheater. While we were waiting in line, a man came up, peered intently into my face, and gruffly informed me, "You've got a good man there." Not knowing who he was, I agreed. "You're right. I'm president of his fan club." The man wasn't satisfied with my response. He bore in more closely and growled, "I SAID, YOU'VE GOT A GOOD MAN THERE," and then abruptly turned on his heel and marched off.

I turned to Les in time to catch the amazed expression on his face. "Who was that guy?" I asked. "That was the admiral," he said disbelievingly.

BULLIES RESPECT ONLY THOSE WHO SAY, "ENOUGH!"

"Sometimes people treat us the way they do not because of the way they are, but because of the way we are." —TONGUE FU'ISM

Bullies push, push, push as a way of taking your measure. They test people to see what they're made of. In a perverse way, they admire only the ones who say, "You're not getting away with that here."

To a bully, silence equals acceptance. Turning the other cheek—hoping verbal abusers will come to their senses, see the error of their ways, apologize, and treat you with more respect—is naive. Appealing to a bully's good nature rarely works; he may not have one.

Although it runs contrary to what you want to do with most people, a good offense is sometimes the best defense when you're dealing with abusive personalities.

I've never told Les's story without someone coming up to me afterward to say, "I worked with someone like that," or "I was married to someone like that." Each say they finally had enough misery and decided not to take it anymore. Each delivered a warning or ultimatum to his or her abuser, and the insults stopped. All were shocked that it was so "easy" to curb the verbal violence they had endured for months or years. Some even reported their persecutor formed a grudging respect and bragged about them to others: "That——, she doesn't take any crap!"

Participants sometimes complain they're powerless to change unfair work situations because the person who is mistreating them controls their career and could cost them their job. I like to tell the story of a secretary who was at her first day on the job when her boss raged into her office and yelled at her for some trivial matter. She drew herself up, pointed him out the door with her finger, and said, *"No one talks to me like that."* She said he meekly left the room and has been treating her courteously all twenty-five years since.

In conclusion, I don't mean to minimize the trauma that bullies can cause, and I certainly don't mean to insinuate that every confrontation with a verbal abuser will turn out like Les's or the secretary's. What I do want to say is that you have a choice in the situation. Instead of accepting the abuse and suffering in silence, consider the risks, speak up for your rights, set boundaries, and take action so you are treated in the way you want and deserve.

ACTION PLAN FOR BREAKING FREE FROM BULLIES

Your older brother used to taunt you when you were kids and has carried this bad habit into adulthood. He frequently belittles you in front of other people. You've never stood up to him before because you were intimidated and didn't want to resort to his tactics, but you've had enough. What do you do?

WORDS TO LOSE	WORDS TO USE
The next time he disparages you, you let him have it with both barrels. *"I'm sick and tired of your picking on me all the time."*	You choose your battles before you confront him so you have evaluated the consequences. *"This is not trivial, it is persistent, and it is intentional."*
You use *I* to preface your statements and come across as weak and whiny. *"Since the time I was five years old, I've had to listen to you say these terrible things about me."*	You use *you* to preface your statements to make him own his unacceptable behavior. *"You need to start treating me with respect, starting today."*
Your brother laughs at you as you tell him what you don't want and how his behavior makes you feel. *"I hate it when you don't take me seriously. I want you to realize how much it hurts me."*	You explain that his behavior will no longer be tolerated. You emphasize what you want and expect from now on. *"You will keep your negative comments to yourself, or you are not welcome in this home."*

· Chapter 27 ·

Give People a Fresh Start

Would you like to know how to let go of grudges?

This idea came from our eight-year-old son Andrew, who got in serious trouble a few years back because he turned our hall wall into a mural. When he emerged from his time-out, he came over to me and circled his toe on the carpet in front of him a few times. I could tell he wanted to make sure he was forgiven and that we still loved him. He finally looked up and asked sweetly, "Mom, can we have a . . . fresh start?" Those simple words have become a tradition in our home—and maybe they can in yours.

When you live and work with people, things go wrong. People lose their temper, say things they wish they hadn't, get irritated, and have bad days. Unless you have a verbal tool to close the books on those conflicts and put them behind you, you end up hauling that harmful history around. You end up dwelling on things that happened weeks, months, years ago. As author David Viscott succinctly observes, "Hurt ages into anger." These grievances accumulate, replace the affection or respect you would otherwise have for this person, and cause *untold* grief.

CLOSE THE BOOK ON CONFLICTS

"I expect to pass through life but once. If therefore, there be any kindness I can show, or any good thing I can do for my fellow being, let me do it now, and not defer or neglect it, as I shall not pass this way again."

—WILLIAM PENN

For your health and that of your loved ones, get rid of those grievances before they bury you in sorrow. Wipe the slate clean and give people a fresh start.

A few weeks after Andrew's artistic adventure, I needed to leave early in the morning to fly from Maui to Honolulu. I called to let the boys know it was time to go, and received no response. I went outside to collect them and found them playing in the yard with the neighbor's pet. They couldn't go to school covered with dog hair and grass stains, so I hustled them inside to change, all the while anxiously checking my watch.

As I was backing the van out of the driveway, Tom yelped, "I forgot my backpack!" By the time he rushed into the house and retrieved it, we were seriously late. I drove like a madwoman because I couldn't afford to miss my plane. I wheeled into the school driveway, braked, and threw open the van door. The boys piled out and I peeled out. I made my flight with only seconds to spare.

On the way home that night, our prop plane flew into a violent thunderstorm, and we were bounced all over the sky. I didn't know if we were going to survive, and all I could think about was the fact that my sons' final memory of me might be of the tense, uptight individual I had been that morning.

As often happens in such situations, I experienced an epiphany ("a sudden . . . perception of the essential nature or meaning of something") and made a pact with God. I vowed if we got back on the ground alive, I would never again part so hurriedly with my family. I would never take for granted a guaranteed next time. I would make each leave-taking one of love rather than helter-skelter haste. Obviously, we landed safe and sound, and that brush with mortality has shaped our good-byes ever since.

Is there someone you were once close to with whom you've

parted on less-than-loving terms? Have you vowed not to apologize because it was "his" fault? Has foolish pride kept you from reapproaching that person? Have you tentatively picked up the phone to call him, and then set it back down because you can't bring yourself to forgive him for his cruel words or deeds?

SUSPEND SPITE

"Pride goeth before destruction, and a haughty spirit before a fall."
—PROVERBS 16:18 IN THE BIBLE

Be honest. Somewhere in your heart, do you assume that someday you'll make up? What if you're robbed of that opportunity? What if something happens to you or the other person in the interim, and you never have a chance to patch things up?

Samuel Butler advised, "Keep your friendships in repair." Part of the Tongue Fu! philosophy is to value your relationships and to take steps to repair those that are broken *now,* not someday. Don't wait or count on some future reunion that may never happen. Henry David Thoreau's last words were "I leave this world without a regret." Could you say the same? If some misunderstanding has resulted in a standoff, transcend your need to be right and let bygones be bygones.

BE WHAT YOU WANT THE WORLD TO BE

"If you see a problem, it's yours. If you think somebody should do something about it, remember, you're as much a somebody as anybody."
—CENTER FOR ZEN BUDDHISM

Are you thinking to yourself, "But they're the ones who started it"? Ask yourself if you'd rather save face or save your friendship. Martin Luther King, Jr., wisely advised, "That old law about 'an eye for an eye' leaves everybody blind." Swallow your pride and be the one to extend the olive branch. Temper is what gets most people in trouble; pride is what keeps them there.

"The final forming of a person's character," Anne Frank believed, "lies in their own hands." Choose to form yourself into a spiritual rather than spiteful person. Say, "Let's not even go into what happened and why. I just want us to be [sisters, brothers, buddies] again. Can we have a fresh start?"

A participant in one of my sessions told me how this idea helped her reunite with her two sisters after ten years of not talking to each other. It's a familiar story. "Our parents left no will. My two older sisters quarreled over who was supposed to be executor and who got what. I didn't want to get drawn into it, but they announced they were going to sell Mom and Dad's home. I couldn't let them do that because our folks had lived in that house for forty years. We each ended up hiring a lawyer to protect our interests. It took two bitter years to resolve the distribution of the estate. By the end, we were communicating only through our attorneys.

"Your story about wondering on that scary airplane ride if you were going to see your kids again made me realize what a risk we were running if something similar happened to one of us and this standoff was still unresolved. I realized how petty we'd been to let this drag on for so long. I called both sisters the night of our class and said *'Don't hang up'* as soon as I identified myself. I asked if we could please put the past in the past and be a family again. Thanks to that story, we are reestablishing those bonds we abandoned so many years ago."

MAINTAIN NO-REGRET RELATIONSHIPS

"Regret for the things we did can be tempered by time; it is regret for the things we did not do that is inconsolable."
—SYDNEY J. HARRIS, AMERICAN NEWSPAPER COLUMNIST

Have you recently had words with a relative or close friend? Or perhaps you've been so busy lately that you haven't had time to get together for that long-anticipated lunch or evening out. Don't wait.

My father died while I was writing this chapter.

A couple of weeks before I started this, our family had reunited in California. For the first time in years, all of my father's children and grandchildren gathered together to celebrate Christmas. I have such a clear image of him sitting on the floor surrounded by his offspring, happily playing Santa and passing out presents. Those few days together were the real gift. We explored Morro Bay by canoe, went horseback riding to the sand dunes, and took our traditional walk/talk. My dad reveled in this opportunity to be a proud patriarch encircled by loved ones in his own home.

When we got back to Hawaii, I promised myself I'd write a note telling Dad what a special time we had. I wanted to make sure he knew how much we appreciated everything he did to make those few days so enjoyable and meaningful. I thought about doing this several times, but there were always other things to do. That thank-you note never got written.

Then I received the phone call about Dad's death. To honor him, I took a long, solitary walk along the beach. I thought back to my earliest memories of him and mentally progressed through his life, cherishing all he had done *for* me and meant *to* me. And I sent that letter to him in my mind.

Who in your life deserves a thank you? What relationship needs repairing? "Peacemaking ultimately must begin at a grassroots level," suggests M. Scott Peck. "It begins with you." Quit procrastinating. Take five minutes now to pick up the phone and reconnect with a friend, or sit down and write that long-overdue appreciation card. You won't regret doing it; you'll only regret *not* doing it.

ACTION PLAN FOR GIVING A FRESH START

Your best friend is moving into a new apartment and asks to use your brand-new van. You agree to let her use it for the weekend to transfer her belongings. She forgets to lock the van, and it is stolen. She has insurance and is apologetic, but it's going to take several weeks of filing claims and police reports before the vehicle can be replaced. How do you handle this?

WORDS TO LOSE	WORDS TO USE
You unleash your anger and let her know exactly how you feel. *"I can't believe you were so careless. How could you have been so stupid as leave the van unlocked?"*	You catch your angry words before they fly so you don't say something you'll regret. *"How did this happen?"*
You focus on this "unforgivable" mistake and the trouble it's going to cause you. *"You'd better call your insurance company, because you're paying for this. My rates aren't going up over your recklessness."*	You realize she's mortified by what happened and that she'd undo it if she could. *"What can be done to rectify this? I'm concerned about the paperwork that needs to be filled out, and a rate increase."*
You refuse to accept her apology. *"Apologizing doesn't do me much good tomorrow morning when I need to drive to work, does it? I wish I'd never let you borrow that van."*	You understand that, as inconvenient as this is going to be, it was an honest mistake. *"If you can get this taken care of, we can put it behind us. Our friendship is more important to me than a car."*

· Chapter 28 ·

Take Charge of Your Emotions!

You may be wondering, "How am I supposed to get someone out of my mind who's done something really terrible to me?"

I'll never forget the first time I showed Eleanor Roosevelt's quote on an overhead transparency during a workshop. I had modified her insight to say, "No one can make us feel *angry* without our consent."

A participant objected, "You have no idea of the kind of people I work with. Do you mean to say if someone is yelling in my face, that's not supposed to make me mad?"

WHO MAKES YOU MAD?

"Control your emotions, or they will control you."

—CHINESE ADAGE

A woman in the same session contributed her opinion: "I agree with Roosevelt's quote because I've lived through it. I'm a surgical nurse. I work with a neurosurgeon who is the most abrasive man I've ever met. He's a brilliant physician, but he has zip people skills.

"Last year I was assisting him in surgery. He asked for a scalpel and I was a fraction of a second late handing it to him. He berated me in front of the rest of the medical staff. He ridiculed me in front of my peers. I was so humiliated, it was all I could do to maintain my professionalism and not walk out of the operating room.

"I started thinking about what he had said to me as I was driving home later that day. By the time I arrived home, I was livid. I started fixing dinner and was slamming the refrigerator door shut and chopping vegetables with a vengeance. I sat down at the dinner table and started telling my husband, Larry, what had happened. Reliving the event got me even more riled up, and I finally erupted with 'That doctor makes me sooo mad!'

"My husband had heard this before. He quietly asked, 'Judy, what time is it?' I looked at him, not sure what he was getting at, and replied, 'It's seven o'clock.' He asked, 'What time did this happen?' 'Nine o'clock this morning,' I told him, still puzzled.

"My husband then wisely pointed out, 'Judy, is it the *doctor* who's making you mad?' and got up from the table and walked out of the room.

"I sat there and thought about it and realized it wasn't the doctor who was making me mad. The doctor wasn't even in the room! I was the one who had given that man a ride home in my car. I was the one who had invited him into my house and set a place for him at our dinner table. I was the one sitting there getting wrapped around the axle about something that had happened ten hours before.

"I decided that evening to never again let that surgeon poison my personal life. From that day forward, I was going to leave him at the hospital. I wasn't going to let him ruin my cherished evenings at home."

WHO IS THE ENEMY?

"Not to have control over the senses is like sailing in a rudderless ship, bound to break to pieces upon coming into contact with the very first rock."
—MAHATMA GANDHI

Who do you bring home with you? Who do you set a place for at your dinner table? A hypercritical boss who notices only what you do wrong and never recognizes all you do right? An uncooperative coworker with a sour attitude? A neighbor incensed about your trees growing over his yard?

According to Sally Kempton, "It is hard to fight an enemy who has outposts in your head." Vow not to let difficult people into your head and into your home, where they have the power to ruin your peace of mind. From now on, take responsibility for your moods instead of turning your tranquillity over to a would-be tormentor.

Charles Darwin observed, "The highest possible stage in moral culture is when we recognize that we ought to control our thoughts." Why dwell on exasperating situations when you can choose instead to focus on other, more pleasant aspects of life?

Psychologists preach that you become what you think about, or as José Ortega y Gasset phrased it, "Tell me to what you pay attention, and I will tell you who you are." If you obsess about the hateful people in your life, you will become a hateful person.

SURROUND YOURSELF WITH A SERENITY SHIELD

"He that respects himself is safe from others; he wears a coat of armor that none can pierce." —HENRY WADSWORTH LONGFELLOW

A young woman volunteered, "I worked for someone like that neurosurgeon. I got a summer job at a factory while I was in college and our floor supervisor did everything she could to make our lives miserable. She'd purposely cut us down with a caustic remark, and if we protested, she'd play innocent and say, 'Can't you take a joke?' or 'I was just kidding.'

"I used to take that woman with me wherever I went. I griped about her to friends, coworkers, anyone who would listen. She was right there beside me on my days off; I even took her along on weekends. Now I see that *she* wasn't making me miserable . . . I was making myself and everyone around me miserable. I was like that cartoon character from the comic strip *Peanuts* who always has a cloud of dust following him—except I had a cloud of disgust following me.

"My dad told me I might as well learn early that it's not realistic to expect to like everyone you work with. He asked if there was anything I could do about her behavior, and I told him it didn't look like it. Several coworkers on my shift had filed complaints, but they weren't given any credence because we were just temporary hires. He told me it was time to put up or shut up—which is just another way of saying choose your battles. I realized I wasn't going to be able to alter her behavior. The union protected her because she had so much seniority. I wasn't willing to quit my job because I needed the money for tuition. So I decided to change myself."

"I put up what I called a serenity shield whenever I was around her. No matter what she said or did, her jabs just bounced harmlessly off that armor. That decision to detach from her cruelty and just do my work as best as I could helped me make the most of that summer instead of moping around."

SQUANDER VS. SAVOR TIME

"Dost thou love life? Then do not squander time, for that is the stuff life is made of."
—BENJAMIN FRANKLIN

A workshop participant named Al wrote to report how he had taken action on this idea. "My wife and I used to take our highly stressful jobs home with us every night. Your workshop helped me realize we weren't enjoying our evenings because all we ever did was gripe about work. We decided to use a modified version of Eleanor Roosevelt's idea to make our home a haven.

"When we get home, we each have fifteen minutes to talk about our day. Then that's it. No more vindictive venting of who did what to whom. We're both in the office and on the road twelve hours a day. That's enough. Why perpetuate the psychic pain? There are lots of other things we can talk about that are infinitely more interesting. We look forward to our evenings now that we've reclaimed them."

PEACE IS AN INSIDE JOB

"Most people are about as happy as they make up their minds to be."
—ABRAHAM LINCOLN

To paraphrase Mr. Lincoln's observation, most people are about as unhappy as they make up their minds to be.

I'll be eternally grateful to a wise tennis coach who opened my eyes to this philosophy. Our team was driving back in our school station wagon from a match in which we had been soundly trounced by our opponents. My fellow players were exchanging war stories about the other team's psych tactics. Our rivals had pulled out all the stops in their efforts to beat us: stalling, calling balls out that were clearly in, talking during crucial points.

All of a sudden our coach veered off the highway into a rest stop, brought the car to a halt, and told us in no uncertain terms to get out. She sat us down on a bench and let us have it. "I've been listening to you ladies moan and groan for the last hour, and I'm sick of it. Stop blaming everybody else for what happened to you. Yes, their players were unfair . . . so is life. You can go around whining and be chumps, or you can *grow up*, and act like champions.

"From now on, no matter what your opponents do, I want you to behave in a way you can be proud. Those teams can't psych you out unless you let them. You lose *only* if they succeed in pulling you down to their level. Now let's get back in the car, and the only thing I want to hear is how you're going to win your next match, and win it like good sports."

"The question is this," says psychologist B. F. Skinner, "are we to be controlled by accidents, by tyrants, or by ourselves?" Stop giving accidents and tyrants the power to make you unhappy, and stop blaming other people or life when things go wrong.

Are you thinking, "That's easy to say and tough to do?" You're right. This has always been and will continue to be one of mankind's eternal challenges. That's why Chapter 29 explores a wide variety of attitude-adjusting philosophies from some of our greatest thinkers. By adopting their wise beliefs or by developing your own, you will be better able to handle life's injustices with grace instead of gripes.

ACTION PLAN FOR TAKING CHARGE OF YOUR EMOTIONS

Your girlfriend dumped you. You can't believe that after two years of dating, she walked away from all you had together. You keep wondering what went wrong, why you didn't see the signals sooner. You're having a hard time putting this behind you, and your self-esteem is almost nonexistent. What do you do?

WORDS TO LOSE	WORDS TO USE
You allow yourself to dwell on what happened and how miserable she made you. *"Didn't she mean all those things she said to me? Was the whole thing a lie? I am so depressed."*	You tell yourself you control your feelings. She can't make you unhappy unless you let her. *"I will focus my attention on all that's right with my world, instead of what's wrong."*
You think how much you miss her and how your life is empty without her. *"What am I going to do Friday night? We always went out someplace special. How could she do this to me?"*	You choose to think about more constructive aspects of your life. *"I'm going to call my college roommate and see if he wants to get together. We always had a good time together."*
You continue to obsess about the relationship and find yourself feeling more and more isolated. *"This would have been our anniversary. I wonder what she's doing tonight?"*	You decide to fill your mind and life with more positive activities. *"I'm glad I'm healthy, that I have a good job and the freedom to do as I please."*

· Chapter 29 ·

Maintain a Positive Perspective

What do you say to yourself when things don't go your way?

Years ago, I was contracted to conduct training for a state organization. The director of the understaffed and overworked division said they were eighteen months behind in the recording and filing of some forms. Every weekday, dozens of people with documents would line up outside, hours before their agency doors even opened. I asked the director how she kept going in the face of such depressing conditions. She said, "You've got to have a philosophy!"

Wise woman. Ever since I had the pleasure of meeting that dedicated manager, I like to ask people, "What's your philosophy?" because I've learned it is a key to the way they experience life. Friedrich Nietzsche noted, "He who has a why to live can bear almost any how." What is your why? You especially need a philosophy to help you deal positively with trying people or times. It's important to reprogram your emotional reflexes so they support rather than sabotage you. When something negative happens, your constructive philosophy kicks in and helps you handle challenges with equanimity rather than irritation.

DOES YOUR PHILOSOPHY SERVE YOU
OR STRESS YOU?

"One's philosophy is not best expressed in words, it is expressed in the choices one makes. In the long run, we shape our lives and we shape ourselves. The process never ends until we die. And the choices we make are ultimately our responsibility." —ELEANOR ROOSEVELT

Victor Frankl survived the Holocaust and wrote about his experiences in the book *Man's Search for Meaning*. This slim volume was selected by the American Library Association as one of the ten most significant books ever written. In it, Frankl concludes that you can't always choose or control what happens to you, you can choose how to respond to it. He certainly didn't choose to be held prisoner in a concentration camp, and he couldn't control what was done to him; he did choose the attitude he took away from that horrific experience. He opted not to harbor hatred. He decided to get on with his life and to dedicate himself to making a positive difference for his fellow human beings.

I introduce Frankl's philosophy in every single Tongue Fu! workshop because I think it's the cornerstone of a mentally healthy lifestyle. You can't always select what happens to you—you might be injured in an automobile accident, a flood could take your home, your job might be eliminated—but you can select how to respond. Little did I know a frightening yet ultimately moving demonstration of this philosophy in action would come from our son, Tom.

To celebrate the last game of the Little League baseball season, our family went to a local restaurant for dinner. We were enjoying the boys' debriefing of their up-to-bats when the waiter reached across our table to refill my coffee. The food server's feet slipped out from underneath him and he spilled the pot of boiling black liquid all over us. I started screaming because I didn't know anything could be that hot. Tom was wailing in pain because the coffee had saturated his baseball pants and was scalding his body.

We quickly removed Tom's clothes, but not before the fluid had stripped the skin off his legs and caused second-degree burns. On the ambulance ride to the hospital, Tom kept crying, "Why me? I wasn't doing anything wrong. Why did this happen?" All we could do was comfort him while the emergency room doctors administered medication and dressed his burns.

Manley Hall pointed out, "A principle is never useful or living or vital until it is embodied in action." That's exactly what Tom did. The day after this unfortunate incident, his younger brother stayed home from school with him (big sacrifice) and spent hours solicitously bringing out games and patiently catering to Tom's every need. The following day Tom received a marvelous packet of letters and drawings from his classmates saying, "We miss you." "Hurry back." "It's no fun without you." It meant so much to Tom to receive this unexpected and welcome affirmation from his peers that he was well liked. And, as Tom tells everyone who will listen, he got to stay home from school for two weeks.

Fortunately, Tom recovered fully with no scars. He now looks back on that experience with the gut knowledge that good things can and do come out of bad things. He will carry that wisdom with him the rest of his years.

"WHY ME?" EQUALS "WOE IS ME"

"Life is like a game of cards. The hand that is dealt you represents determinism; the way you play it is free will."

—JAWAHAREAL NEHRU

When things go wrong, the universal almost automatic reaction is "Why me?" If you continue to lament your fate with angry entreaties—"I don't deserve this," "This isn't fair"—you will continue to feel victimized. You will see the world as a harsh environment where innocent people are besieged by bad things.

You can play a "poor hand of cards" more positively by asking, "Where's the good?" One of life's most important insights is to know with your heart and soul, as Tom now does, that good things can come out of bad. This is not to say that bad things are good. You may have been presented with bleak circumstances that were in no way positive, but you can reap positive things as a result of them. The good may not always be apparent at the time. If you search for it, it will emerge.

In his thought-provoking book *No Ordinary Moments,* author Dan Millman postulates that the issues we face are the spiritual weights we lift to strengthen ourselves. He believes our task is to shine *through* the petty details of our life, not become preoccupied with them. He says, "At the moment of your death, your whole life will pass before you. In a few fractions of a second—because time no longer applies—you will see many incidents from your life in order to learn. You will review your life with two questions in your consciousness: Could I have shown a little more courage in these moments? Could I have shown a little more love?"

Over the years, my audiences have contributed dozens of different philosophies that have helped them handle adversity with courage and love. A fellow trainer reacts to disappointments with a lilting "Oh well," and she's off to other activities. One woman whose parents operated a deli said her mother taught her to pity rude customers ("Isn't it too bad they didn't have parents who taught them better manners?") rather than punish them ("It's going to be a long time before they get their sandwich").

For many people, the guideline that governs their actions is the Golden Rule, "Do unto others as you would have them do unto you." In her book *Feel the Fear and Do It Anyway,* Susan Jeffers recommends that you repeat the words "I can handle it" whenever you encounter adversity. This phrase works as a mantra you can use to calm yourself in the face of threatening circumstances. Those four words create a feeling of confidence ("I can") rather than cynicism ("I can't").

Ann Landers advises her readers to "expect trouble as an inevitable part of life and repeat to yourself the most comforting words of all: This, too, shall pass." Despair is defined as the "utter loss of hope." Instead of wallowing in despair when things go wrong, people must remember that their trials are temporary and that they have plenty of reasons to hope for better tomorrows.

LOOK AT ADVERSITY WITH A WIDE-ANGLE LENS

"We can choose to see life as a series of trials and tribulations, or we can choose to see life as an accumulation of treasures." —ANONYMOUS

Would you like to know how to get instant perspective if you're feeling down? Understand that anytime you're feeling troubled, you usually have your mental telephoto lens focusing exclusively on your trials and tribulations. You are obsessing about a difficult person or disturbing situation. You can almost immediately change your attitude by switching to a wide-angle lens and focusing on all that's *right* with your world instead of what's wrong. Instead of obsessing about your ordeal, you become aware of the abundance surrounding you.

Are you thinking, "Sounds good in theory, but it's tough to put into practice?" You're right, so I've developed a more tangible method to help you keep your mental wide-angle lens focused on your accumulation of treasures.

WAKE UP TO WONDERS

"The universe is full of magical things patiently waiting for our wits to grow sharper." —EDEN PHILLPOTTS

Buy a beautiful calendar and hang it in your kitchen. By sharpening your wits to the magical things around you, you can compensate for the injustices you endure. Resolve to write down one thing that goes right every day. Log a laugh you shared over breakfast, an invigorating walk you took at sunrise, a credit card bill you finally paid off, a funny remark you overheard, the glory of a spring day, a landmark occasion, or an inspiring movie. Just take ten seconds to record something that went well today.

As Frank Lloyd Wright commented, "If you foolishly ignore beauty, you'll soon find yourself without it. Your life will be impoverished. But if you wisely invest in beauty, it will remain with you all the days of your life." Record the beauty in your world, and it can indeed remain with you all your days.

In his insightful audiotape *Happiness Is a Serious Problem,* Dennis Prager shares a surprising revelation. After years of research on this topic, he's concluded there is only one thing that makes people happy. Think about it. Money does not make people happy. Neither does fame. All you have to do is read *People* to know that more than a few wealthy celebrities are forlorn. Even love and good health don't necessarily make people happy.

A sense of *gratitude* is the only direct determinant of happiness. As Prager points out, gratitude is a state of mind you can maintain regardless of your circumstances. You can have everything but be miserable if you don't value what you have. You can have very little yet be content if you're appreciative for what you do have. It's very straightforward—the more gratitude you have, the happier you'll be. The less gratitude you have, the less happy you'll be.

If you invest the time to make daily entries into your Calendar of Comments, do you know what you'll have as the weeks and months go by? You'll have:

- a written record of your accumulation of treasures
- evidence of everything that's right with your world
- a visual legacy of all for which you have to be grateful
- a permanent keepsake of your beautiful moments

Mother Teresa once quipped, "I know God will not give me anything I can't handle. I just wish He didn't trust me so much." If life is giving you a lot to handle, your calendar of treasures can help you focus on life's marvels instead of its miseries.

HARD TIMES VS. HAPPY TIMES

"Good memories are our second chance at happiness."
—QUEEN ELIZABETH II

If you're a parent, you've undoubtedly learned you can't control your children's lives, nor can you choose everything that happens to them. You can give them happy memories; you can create good times to offset the hard times. Aristotle wisely advised, "Happiness depends on ourselves." Happiness can depend on prominently displaying and maintaining a Calendar of Comments in your home so you have an ever-present reminder of your blessings vs. your burdens.

If you're lucky, your kids will suggest, "Let's read the calendar after dinner," and you'll have second and third chances to relive your happy moments. One of our favorite entries was made on a Christmas Day. Andrew tore into a beautifully wrapped present and cheered with delight upon discovering a motorized truck. After several minutes spent unsuccessfully trying to start it, he pouted, "It's not working!" Brother Tom patiently explained, "Of *course* it's not working. You forgot to read the *de*-structions."

COUNTERBALANCE CORPORATE CALAMITIES

"If you are distressed by anything external, the pain is not due to the thing itself, but to your estimate of it; and this you have the power to revoke at any moment."
—MARCUS AURELIUS

If you work in an office, buy another calendar and post it where everyone has access to it. Ask your coworkers to rotate responsibility for making daily entries. Record a contract your company won, a surprise birthday party for your supervisor, a customer who called to say thank you, a major project that was completed on time, an award given for outstanding service.

When setbacks occur, when you encounter difficult clients, when the computer breaks down, look at the calendar to remember your triumphs instead of these tests of patience. This calendar can help your work team concentrate on their accomplishments rather than their annoyances. It serves as a counterbalance to the crises that can be an everyday part of the corporate world. Pull it out once a month at staff meetings to remind employees they are making progress, that they are making a difference, and that their work matters.

ACTION PLAN FOR MAINTAINING A POSITIVE PERSPECTIVE

You drive to your bank to get some cash only to discover there's been a power outage. The doors are closed, and the automatic teller machine is shut down. How do you react to this inconvenience?

WORDS TO LOSE	WORDS TO USE
You react to the situation with frustration. *"I made this trip for nothing."*	You have a philosophy that kicks in when things go wrong. *"I can handle this. This is not that big a deal."*
Your negative thoughts continue to sabotage you. *"This is going to mess up my whole afternoon. What am I supposed to do, wait around for them to fix it?"*	Your positive thoughts serve you. *"Oh well, maybe I could use another bank machine and get cash from my credit card instead."*
You dwell on the trouble this causes you and stay bothered. *"I hate it when things like this happen. Like I've got time on my hands . . ."*	You expect trouble as a part of life and realize it's temporary. *"This too shall pass. I won't even remember this a year from now. I'll run some other errands."*
You keep your mental telephoto lens focused on this trial. *"I'm going to complain to the bank about this. Why don't they have a generator?"*	You switch to a wide-angle lens and gain instant perspective. *"Look around. There's lots right with my life. I have much to be grateful for."*

· Chapter 30 ·

Ki 'Em with Kindness

Have you heard the phrase "kill 'em with kindness?"

I believe that saying is an oxymoron, a "combination of contradictory or incongruous words (as *cruel kindness*)." Kindness and killing are indeed contradictory and incongruous.

A more appropriate approach to dealing with people is encapsulized in the title of this chapter, "Ki 'Em with Kindness."

Whatever your belief or religion, you probably have a word for your spirit. In Japan, this invisible life force is called *ki* (pronounced key). The Chinese call this energy *chi* (pronounced chee). Martial artists believe there is plus ki and minus ki, and that we constantly choose which to exude. The more positive your ki, the less susceptible you are to other people's negative energy. How can you develop a strong spirit so you can be, as Luke Skywalker said in the popular movie *Star Wars,* a force for the good side rather than the dark?

You can put the Pygmalion Principle (sometimes referred to as the Boomerang Law) to work *for* you rather than *against* you. This concept postulates that "what you give is what you get." If you treat people with suspicion and contempt (dark or minus ki), they will treat you the same way. Their surly reaction will prove your perception, which will perpetuate your attitude, which will provide more evidence of your view that the world is hostile . . . and the pessimistic spiral will continue.

Conversely, if you treat people with dignity and respect (light or plus ki), they are more likely to reciprocate *in kind*. Their friendly reaction will reinforce your belief the world is a caring place, which will support and encourage your behavior, and the optimistic spiral will continue upward.

THE KI CROSSROADS

"Peace of mind means the ability to be organized inwardly; it means inner tranquility in the midst of confusion, difficulty, conflict, or opposition."
—NORMAN VINCENT PEALE

How can you apply this principle in everyday life? By visualizing yourself standing at a ki crossroads whenever you encounter adversity. You can take the low road or you can take the high road. You have at best a few seconds to decide which path to take.

If you allow yourself to react and say even a few mean-spirited words, you'll already be on the downward path, with your words propelling you ever faster. This route is sometimes easier and more tempting to take. However, the trail descends rapidly, your minus ki gaining momentum and hurtling you downward to the dark side of the human soul.

If you can manage to think or speak a few charitable words about what's happened (here's where your ingrained compassionate philosophy comes in), you've set a more positive course of action and your plus ki will elevate you above the fray. This path often requires more effort, but the view you get when you come out on top, above it all, is worth the climb.

Ideally, your pledge to project peacefulness would prevent people from treating you unkindly. Cicero himself said, "Persistent kindness conquers the ill-disposed." Realistically, you know that won't always happen. The good news is that whether or not you favorably affect the person with whom you're dealing, your personal vow to behave honorably is self-rewarding.

Kurt Vonnegut has written that "we are healthy only to the extent that our ideas are humane." By choosing to be humanitarian rather than hostile, you reap a centered state that is *nonsituational.* Tranquil is defined as "free from agitation of mind or spirit." Your mind and spirit can remain free of agitation if you choose to extend positive energy, no matter what. In this way, your peace of mind doesn't depend on where you are, who you're with, or what is happening—you carry it with you wherever you go.

CONSTANT KINDNESS

"No act of kindness, no matter how small, is ever wasted." —AESOP

Life saw fit to put me to the test to see just how firmly I believed this concept of tranquility. I had just finished a Tongue Fu! workshop and a gentleman approached me with a well-meaning compliment: "I love that story about the nurse and the neurosurgeon. It's even better the second time around."

"Oh," I commented, "you've attended one of my seminars before?"

"No," he replied, "a speaker told that same story, almost word for word, at our state convention last month. In fact, her presentation was very similar to yours. She talked about the AAA Train, Words to Lose/Use, and Tactful Termination, too."

I was upset. Those were *my* stories and ideas. I spent a lot of time developing and fine-tuning them. The *nerve* of this person to use them and not give me credit. Distressed, I called a fellow speaker that evening and asked for advice.

Maggie said, "Sam, you've got to decide how you're going to handle this because it happens a lot in our business." She asked, "How many speeches do you give a year?" "About seventy-five," I answered. "How many people are in your audience on the average?" "Anywhere from thirty to three thousand," I estimated. Maggie added it up and concluded, "That means at least twenty-five thousand people hear your information annually. You have to expect that some of them are going to take your techniques and call them their own. You can choose to chase 'em all down and read them the riot act, or you can wish them well.

"Why are you in this business?" Maggie asked. "To make a positive difference for as many people as possible," I replied. "Then," she reasoned, "if someone tells your story and people benefit from hearing it, isn't that what you want? You can choose to be stingy and proprietary, but that will just make you neurotic. You'll worry constantly that someone's out there lifting your ideas.

"Why don't you choose instead to come from a place of abundance? Be generous with your material. *Encourage* people to pass it on. In the long run, it's a better way to be."

I've had several occasions since then to practice what Maggie preached (all speakers and writers do), and she was right. No matter what your occupation or line of work, there will always be unscrupulous people who'll steal your stuff. If you take the low road and obsess about it, you'll end up making yourself miserable and you'll waste valuable time embroiled in petty ownership battles. Instead, take the high road, *share* your stuff, concentrate on adding value, and maintain an attitude of "goodwill toward men." As Maggie wisely observed, it's a better way to be.

EXTEND ALOHA

"A loving heart is the truest wisdom."   —CHARLES DICKENS

Hawaiians have a unique way of describing goodwill: they call it aloha. Aloha, often used in Hawaii as a warm greeting or fond farewell, means an "unselfish, benevolent concern for the good of another." Aloha is unconditional love. Marie Curie believed that "you cannot hope to build a better world without improving the individuals. To that end, each of us must work for our own improvement, and at the same time share a general responsibility for all humanity, our particular duty being to aid those to whom we think we can be more useful."

Mae, a self-described burnt-out bus driver, paid her own money to take my Tongue Fu! workshop because she was worried she wasn't going to be able to hang in there until her retirement, three years off. She confessed, "I need this class. I am sick and tired of people asking me for quarters when there's a sign posted right in front of them that says we don't give change. I'll be driving in rush-hour traffic and someone will push a map in my face and ask for directions. We don't allow backpacks or strollers, and people yell at me because they can't bring them on board. Teenagers play those huge boom boxes and dare me to try to stop them. What am I supposed to do? It's a zoo."

Toward the end of the seminar, after we had talked about Victor Frankl's philosophy and the Pygmalion Principle, this longtime city employee walked up and said, "I can't remember exactly when I abandoned the aloha spirit, but I don't like what I've become. I know how to stop my passengers from being so rude. *I'm* going to stop being rude to them."

Mae was thoughtful enough to send a follow-up letter updating me on her progress. "I used to have to drag myself to work in the morning; now I look forward to it. I started wearing a fresh flower lei to work, and sometime during the day I give it away to someone who looks like they could use it. Yesterday I draped it around the neck of an older woman who always rides by herself. She said she felt like 'Queen for a Day' and that it had been years since anyone had given her a present. The day before, I gave it to a Japanese couple who asked another passenger to take a picture of them with the 'friendly bus driver.' Those leis have become a symbol for me. They remind me to act with aloha . . . and you know what, it *does* come back."

As this woman bus driver so delightfully discovered, the best way to change how people treat you is to change how you treat them. Her choice to extend aloha enriched her world and the world of everyone she touches.

HOW TO CREATE A COCOON OF KINDNESS

"If you want a quality, act as if you already had it. Try the 'as if'
technique."   —WILLIAM JAMES

Not sure you can achieve this charity of spirit? As the famous Nike
ad suggests, "Just do it!"

In the beginning, there's no substitute for simply monitoring
your actions to see if they're "naughty or nice." If what you were
going to say or do is not magnanimous, then maintain your silence.
Magnanimity is defined as "loftiness of spirit, nobility of feeling,
and generosity of mind enabling one to bear trouble calmly, to dis-
dain meanness and revenge, and to make sacrifices for worthy ends."

Wow. That's some definition. Please read it again, because it
summarizes what Tongue Fu! is all about. Resolve to replace less-
than-charitable thoughts with your personal philosophy. Drown
out vindictive reactions by substituting, "I choose to be kind," or
"I will remain calm and compassionate." Fill your mind with how
you want to behave rather than indulging in spiteful feelings.

A yoga teacher uses the "as if" technique for achieving a state of
tranquility. This woman, who radiates a serene spirit, has modeled
herself after her sensei (wise teacher, literally "one who is born before"). She said whenever she is troubled, she asks herself how this
sensei would react, then acts as he would. She noticed that he never
got ruffled; he always seemed to be in a state of grace. Grace is defined as "ease of bearing, the quality or state of being considerate
and thoughtful, a disposition of kindness." She had always heard
the expression "fall out of grace," and she decided her philosophy
was going to be the opposite: she was going to "fall into grace."

Modeling yourself after an admired mentor is a time-tested way
to hasten the acquiring of a skill. Yogi Berra said (as only he could),
"You can observe a lot just by watching." You can *learn* a lot just
by watching someone who is the picture of poise. Who do you
know who manages to keep cool under fire? If you are dealing with
a difficult situation, adopt his or her approach and act as they
would.

CULTIVATE YOUR KI

"What do you think of Western civilization?"

—REPORTER'S QUESTION

"I think it's a good idea."   —MAHATMA GANDHI'S ANSWER

An engineer in one of my workshops spoke up and said, "This sounds a little New Agey to me. Don't you have some practical methods we can use to keep our blood pressure from boiling?"

Good question. Learning yoga, practicing meditation, and studying the gentle martial art of aikido are all excellent ways to develop a peaceful spirit. There are two other specific techniques you can use to stay calm in moments of chaos.

It's said, "The best cure for a short temper is a long walk." If you're about to lose your temper and you can't take a long walk, take a long breath. Shallow, irregular breathing creates a panicky, confused state of mind. Yoga masters and martial artists learn to breathe rhythmically and deeply so they can take charge of their ki and their temperament. They know if they're out of breath, they'll be out of sorts, and they'll soon be out of control.

You can learn to belly-breathe with five minutes of concentrated practice each day. Find a quiet place and remove distractions. Commit to focusing full attention on your exchange of air. When inhaling, draw in the oxygen through your nose for four beats while filling out your stomach. Then, as aikido master Tohei suggests, "breathe out so your breath travels to the shores of heaven. At first, you may be uncomfortable, but if you continue this exercise, you will reach the stage where you forget your own body and enter into a peaceful world of nothing but breathing."

Are you wondering how this can help you deal with a threatening situation? Belly-breathing is a tangible tool for counteracting the natural fight-or-flight response. Ritualized breathing relaxes you physically (your pulse rate and blood pressure will drop) and mentally (your mind will steady and become quiet). If you're skeptical, just try it. You have nothing to lose, except fear itself.

BECOME ONE WITH YOUR ONE POINT

"Each one has to find his peace from within. And peace to be real must be unaffected by outside circumstances." —MAHATMA GANDHI

Martial artists know that if they're "in their head," they will feel scatterbrained and unstable. If they react from the neck up when they are attacked, they'll be mentally and physically unbalanced and will be vulnerable to more powerful forces.

Instead, they learn to move their consciousness down and "think in their abdomen." From ancient times, the pit of the stomach, also known as the one point, has been thought to be the birthplace of true human strength. When you maintain your one point, you feel centered and firmly rooted. This may sound esoteric, but martial artists have practiced it for thousands of years, and it is the essence of their ability to remain composed and focused in the most dire of circumstances.

Perhaps you've seen a demonstration of this. A martial artist will invite a couple members of the audience up to the stage and ask them to try to push him off balance or to lift him up. This is a relatively easy task at first because the demonstrator does not employ his one point. The participants can make the instructor take a step back with a simple thrust of their finger, or two participants can lift him up with very little effort.

Then the master moves his mind down to and lets his weight settle in his hara (another term for the body's center of gravity in the lower abdomen). He stands so solidly that the members of the audience are unable to push him over or lift him off the floor, even when applying all their strength.

You don't have to be trained in martial arts to discover how to become one with your one point. My sons were able to learn this in their first aikido lesson. Amazed at the simplicity of the concept and in awe of its ramifications, they said in wonderment, "It really works!" They couldn't wait to take this back to school so they wouldn't be bowled over by playground bullies. By centering themselves, they could keep from being pushovers and from being knocked down by big kids looking for trouble.

From now on when you're faced with a challenge, combine the physical act of belly breathing with the mental act of centering yourself in your one point, and combine those with your spiritual resolve to extend aloha. By choosing to ki people with kindness, regardless of how they're treating you, *you're* deciding the way you want to be in this world, rather than letting others determine that for you. Thomas Carlyle concluded that "without kindness, there can be no true joy." Your commitment to be a spiritual force for good will positively influence your every encounter, and will create more joy in your life on a daily basis.

ACTION PLAN FOR KI 'EM WITH KINDNESS

A cranky lady in your building seems perpetually mad at the world. Her crabby attitude gets a little hard to take, and sometimes you get an uncharitable urge to tell her to shut up. You avoid her whenever possible, but she occasionally corners you in the hall or on the elevator. How do you choose to treat this (as Cicero would say) "ill-disposed" person?

WORDS TO LOSE	WORDS TO USE
You feel contempt for her behavior, and it is evident in your response to her. *"What a witch. She could make a rabbit bite."*	You choose to treat her with courtesy even if she doesn't return it. *"I will remain kind and compassionate—no matter what."*
You set up a negative boomerang effect by "putting *her* in her place." *"Lady, you are the most unpleasant person I've ever met. Why don't you get a life and stop taking your . . ."*	You set up a positive boomerang effect by putting *yourself* in her place. *"I'll bet she doesn't have any friends, and that she's lonely."*
You let her affect you, react with minus ki, and feed the hostility. *"I'm not going to stand here and listen to this garbage. Why don't you just keep your complaints to yourself?"*	You maintain your cocoon of kindness and continue to extend positive ki. *"I will stay centered by breathing slowly and deeply. I choose to be a person of aloha."*

> "PEOPLE ARE ALWAYS BLAMING THEIR
> CIRCUMSTANCES FOR WHAT THEY ARE. I DON'T
> BELIEVE IN CIRCUMSTANCES. THE PEOPLE WHO GET
> ON IN THIS WORLD ARE THE PEOPLE WHO GET UP
> AND LOOK FOR THE CIRCUMSTANCES THEY WANT,
> AND, IF THEY CAN'T FIND THEM, MAKE THEM."
> —GEORGE BERNARD SHAW

· Epilogue ·
Turn Intentions Into Actions

Have you ever finished a book all fired up, ready to go out and change the world, and two weeks later everything was back to "same old same old"? Please don't let that happen with this book.

My business is called Action Seminars because I believe the object of education isn't knowledge, it's action. Information is not power unless it's used.

Are you thinking, "I don't know where to start?" Confusion immobilizes. Clarity leads to action. The purpose of this last section is to help you clarify your priorities so you can put them into action.

IDENTIFY PRIORITIES

"If you don't know where to begin, you don't begin."
—GENERAL GEORGE S. PATTON

Certainly you can't master all these suggestions all at once. A more reasonable goal is to select two of the most important concepts, write exactly how you plan to use them, and post this reminder in a prominent place so you are frequently reminded of your commitment to adopt new communication customs.

As Henry Ford, the father of the assembly line, observed, "Nothing is particularly hard if you divide it up." You can become a Tongue Fu! black belt if you incorporate these techniques into your daily life in small increments.

Please review this book. Skim through the pages and pick two ideas particularly timely and relevant for you. Write why you like the idea (e.g., "I like the idea about reflecting rather than refuting because it will help me be a better listener to my kids"). If this is a library book, you can duplicate these pages and fill them out, or create your own action plan on the inside front cover of your Tongue Fu! calendar.

PRIORITY IDEA 1

I like _____

_____

because _____

_____

_____

PRIORITY IDEA 2

I like _____

_____

because _____

_____

_____

TURN KNOWLEDGE INTO POWER

"Knowing is not enough, we must apply. Willing is not enough, we must do."
—JOHANN GOETHE

Now write exactly how you're going to put these principles into practice. For example, "I'm going to say 'What do you mean?' when I don't know what to say so I don't say something I regret." Or "Instead of explaining what went wrong, I'm going to take the AAA Train when someone's complaining." Or "I'm going to adopt as a philosophy, 'I will keep my sense of humor—no matter what!—so people don't have the power to ruin my day.' "

Be sure to include all the Ws (Who, What, When, Why and Where). The more specific you are in outlining your action plan, the more likely you will implement it.

ACTION PLAN FOR PRIORITY 1: I'm going to _____
_____
_____
_____
_____
_____

ACTION PLAN FOR PRIORITY 2: I'm going to _____
_____
_____
_____
_____
_____

PERSEVERE THROUGH PESSIMISM

"Nothing is impossible to the willing mind."
—BOOKS OF HAN DYNASTY

Are you thinking, "I'm not sure I can change my habits?" Helen Keller knew from experience that "We can do anything we want as long as we stick to it long enough."

I'll always remember the time I was presenting a workshop and we had just finished discussing Words to Lose/Use. A man shakily raised his hand as we completed the list of trigger words and said, "I use those words all the time! I used 'em all in one *sentence* this morning!"

He elaborated, "I told my head engineer he had to work over-time this weekend to repair some electrical problems. He said he couldn't because his parents were arriving from out of town and they had made plans. I told him, "Well, I'm sorry you've got a *problem* with working this weekend, *but* you're going to *have to* because you're the only one who knows the system. You *should* have told me earlier you couldn't come in. *There's nothing* I can do about it now. I *can't* ask anyone else *because* they're not familiar with the system.""

He shook his head remorsefully. "We really got into it. What am I supposed to do though, write these words on my palm? I can't remember all these dos and don'ts."

He's right: it can be a challenge to change deeply ingrained habits. I asked the class if they'd be willing to try an exercise that demonstrates the three-step process to picking up new skills. If you will take thirty seconds to complete this simple assignment, you too can overcome any skepticism you might have.

THE THREE A'S TO ACQUIRING SKILLS

"If at first you don't succeed, you're about average." —ANONYMOUS

Please write, using your best handwriting, the sentence "I'm good at Tongue Fu!" (Once again, if this is a library book, please use an-other piece of paper.)

Now write the same sentence with your other hand.

How did it feel to write with your other hand? How does that sec-ond sentence look? Most people agree that writing with the nondominant hand is time-consuming and uncomfortable.

What is the point? Would you agree that handwriting is a skill? How about tennis? Using the computer? Sure, they all are. People aren't born knowing how to do these things. They have to learn them step by step. In the mastery of any skill, people go through three stages. While you were writing that second sentence, you experienced firsthand the initial stage of adopting new habits. Interestingly, the three stages of learning all start with the letter A.

> **A = Awkward.** When you try something new or different, you usually don't do it very well. Remember the first time you drove a car with a gearshift? Did you give yourself a mild case of whiplash from starting, stopping, and stalling? Instead of giving up in frustration ("I'll never do that again"), you reassured yourself that poor performance was to be expected ("Of course I didn't drive very well. I'd never done it before"). You wanted to acquire this skill, so you kept practicing, which advanced you to the next stage of learning.

> **A = Applying.** At this stage, you are applying the techniques you've been taught and getting improved results. You're coordinating the gas pedal, brake, and clutch while smoothly moving the stick shift. You're able to get through an intersection and turn corners without causing an accident. You want to become an even better driver, so you continue to practice the fundamentals.

> **A = Automatic.** At this point, you don't even have to think about what you're doing because it comes so naturally. You're an experienced driver who gets from Point A to Point B while having conversations and playing the radio—all safely and without a moment's thought as to the process that's producing your performance. The fundamentals are performed unconsciously and effectively.

PRACTICE AND PATIENCE PAYS OFF

"Failure is the path of least persistence."　　　　—ANONYMOUS

Are you wondering, "What's this got to do with Tongue Fu?" Wouldn't you agree that Tongue Fu! is a skill? As with any skill, it takes time to master. It may feel awkward using *and* at first instead of *but.* You may feel uncomfortable speaking up for what you want because you've got a history of going along to get along. You may occasionally lose your temper and forget your good intentions to be compassionate. That doesn't mean you've failed. That doesn't mean Tongue Fu! doesn't work or that you can't learn it. It just means you're in the natural first stages of changing old habits and acquiring new ones.

Satchel Paige quipped, "Sometimes you win, sometimes you lose, sometimes you get rained out." Don't give up in those initial *awkward* stages when you get less-than-perfect results. Persevere. Be patient with yourself and continue to apply the techniques you've discovered in this book. You'll find yourself becoming more confident when confronted with difficult people. You'll get to the point where your Tongue Fu! skills automatically switch on in stressful situations.

TONGUE FU! IS A BY-PRODUCT

"Happiness isn't a goal. It's a by-product."　　—ELEANOR ROOSEVELT

Tongue Fu! isn't a goal, it's a by-product of following up and using the ideas covered in this book. I realize there's a lot to digest, so I've created an acronym to help you remember eight crucial concepts that can help you turn conflicts into cooperation.

T = Therapist's tool. . . .	Reflect, don't refute. Listen, don't lecture.
O = Open mind	Give people a chance and a fresh start.
N = Needs	Keep the scale in balance and say no.
G = Gracefully exit	End arguments with "Let's not do this."
U = Understand	Turn anger into empathy with "How would I feel?"
E = End complaints	Don't explain, take the AAA train.
F = Friendly phrases . . .	Turn resentment into rapport with Words to Use
U = Use your philosophy	Maintain a positive perspective—no matter what!

RECIPES DON'T MAKE COOKIES

"To change one's life, start immediately, do it flamboyantly, no exceptions."
—WILLIAM JAMES

I know this cookbook of conflict resolution recipes works if *you* will! According to Thomas Edison, "Our greatest weakness lies in giving up. The most certain way to succeed is to always try just one more time." I hope you always try to diplomatically disarm difficult people, and that you never give up your commitment to ki people with kindness.

As Adlai Stevenson advised, "Knowledge alone is not enough.

It must be leavened with magnanimity before it becomes wisdom." John Ruskin noted something similar when he observed, "When love and skill go together, expect a masterpiece."

I hope you will practice these Tongue Fu! skills on a daily basis and that you will wisely leaven them with a loving spirit of magnanimity. If you do, you can become a master of peace.

· Postscript ·

Have you developed a response (Tongue Fu'ism) that has helped you deflect, defuse, or disarm a difficult person? Do you have a success story (Tongue Fu! Coup) you'd like to share with me and/or with future readers? Is there a dreaded question or challenging scenario you'd like discussed in my next book, *Tongue Fu II*?

My favorite quote comes from Leo Rosten. "The purpose of life isn't to be happy. It's to matter; to feel it's made some difference you have lived at all." It means a lot to me to receive your feedback and to know how these ideas have made a difference for you. I realize you're busy, so thank you in advance for taking the time to contribute your Tongue Fu! treasures. Please include your mailing address and a telephone, FAX, or E-mail number. If your example is featured in a future *Tongue Fu!* book, I want to be able to get back in touch with you to verify the material and to ask for permission to use it.

You are invited to visit my WEBsite or to contact me at the following addresses for information about a free sample newsletter, other books, audio- and videotapes, training programs for your organization, and a schedule of upcoming public appearances. I look forward to hearing from you. Mahalo!

Hawaii Office
Sam Horn
P.O. Box 959
Kihei, HI 96753-0959
1 (808) 879-5661 or FAX (808) 879-0441

U.S. Mainland Office
Cheri Grimm, Manager
P.O. Box 6810
Los Osos, CA 93412-6810
1 (800) 726-3455

E-mail: infor@samhorn.com *and* order@samhorn.com
WEBsite: http://www.bookfair.com/welcome/tonguefu/book

· Recommended Reading ·

Ailes, R. *You Are the Message.* Homewood, Ill.: Dow Jones-Irwin, 1988.

Bach, G., and P. Wyden. *The Intimate Enemy.* New York: Avon Books, 1968.

Bedrosian, M. *Life Is More Than Your To-Do List.* Rockville, Md.: BCI Press, 1994.

Boettinger, H. *Moving Mountains: The Art of Letting Others See Things Your Way.* New York: Collier Books, 1969.

Borysenko, J. *Minding the Body, Mending the Mind.* New York: Bantam Books, 1987.

Bolton, R. *People Skills.* Englewood Cliffs, N.J.: Prentice-Hall, 1979.

Booher, D. *Communicate with Confidence.* New York: McGraw-Hill, 1994.

Cramer, K. *Staying on Top When Your World Turns Upside Down.* New York: Viking Penguin, 1990.

Charles, L. *Stick to It!* East Lansing, Mich.: Trainingworks, 1994.

Crum, T. *The Magic of Conflict.* New York: Touchstone, 1987.

DeAngelis, B. *Real Moments.* New York: Delacorte Press, 1994.

Deshimaru, T. *The Zen Way to the Martial Arts.* New York: Arkana Penguin, 1982.

Faber, A., and E. Mazlish. *How to Talk So Kids Will Listen & Listen So Kids Will Talk.* New York: Avon Books, 1980.

Fisher, R., and W. Ury. *Getting to Yes.* Boston: Houghton Mifflin Company, 1981.

Gray, J. *Men Are from Mars, Women Are from Venus.* New York: HarperCollins, 1992.

Hyams, J. *Zen in the Martial Arts.* New York: Bantam Books, 1979.

Jeffers, S. *Feel the Fear and Do It Anyway.* New York: Fawcett Columbine, 1987.

Klein, A. *The Healing Power of Humor.* Los Angeles: Jeremy Tarcher, 1989.

Laborde, G. *Influencing with Integrity.* Palo Alto, Calif.: Syntony Publishing, 1983.

LeBoeuf, M. *How to Win Customers and Keep Them for Life.* New York: Berkley, 1988.

McWilliams, J. and P. *You Can't Afford the Luxury of a Negative Thought.* Los Angeles: Prelude Press, 1988.

Millman, D. *No Ordinary Moments.* Tiburon, Calif.: H. J. Kramer, 1992.

Nierenberg, G. *The Art of Negotiating.* New York: Cornerstone Library, 1968.

Pater, R. *The Black-Belt Manager.* Rochester, Vt.: Park Street Press, 1988.

Pearson, J. *Interpersonal Communication.* Glenview, Ill.: Scott, Foresman, 1983.

Pelley, J. *Laughter Works.* Fair Oaks, Calif.: Laughter Works Seminars, 1994.

Redfield, J. *The Celestine Prophecy.* New York: Warner, 1993.

Robbins, A. *Unlimited Power.* New York: Fawcett Columbine, 1987.

Safransky, S., ed. *Sunbeams: A Book of Quotations.* Berkeley: North Atlantic Books, 1990.

Sarnoff, D. *Never Be Nervous Again.* New York: Ballantine, 1987.

Scheele, A. *Skills for Success.* New York: Ballantine, 1979.

Tannen, D. *You Just Don't Understand.* New York: William Morrow, 1990.

Tohei, K. *Ki in Daily Life.* Tokyo: Ki No Kenkyukai H.Q., 1978.